World Snooker
with Jack Karnehm
No. 2

PELHAM BOOKS

ACKNOWLEDGEMENTS

We would like to thank Jean and Lesley for their fortitude, the Billiards and Snooker Control Council, Roy Couch, John Marchant and all the people in the world of snooker who helped to make this book possible.

Jack Karnehm
John Carty

First published in Great Britain by
PELHAM BOOKS LTD
44 Bedford Square
London WC1B 3DU
1982

Copyright © Jack Karnehm and John Carty 1982

All Rights Reserved. No part of this publication may be reproduced, stored in a retrieval system, or transmitted, in any form or by any means, electronic, mechanical, photocopying, recording or otherwise without the prior permission of the Copyright owner.

British Library Cataloguing in Publication Data

World snooker.—No. 2
  1. Snooker—Periodicals
  794.7'35'05   GV900.S6
  ISBN 0-7207-1398-6

Filmset by Rowland Phototypesetting Ltd
Bury St Edmunds, Suffolk

Printed in Great Britain by
Penshurst Press Limited,
Tunbridge Wells

Cover photographs by Dave Muscroft

Contents

	Preface	5
1	My Crucible view	6
2	The Supreme Snooker League	14
3	What the heck do they mean?	20
4	The Karnehm method	25
5	Meet the new professionals	33
6	Rules is rules	40
7	The turning point	46
8	Such stuff as dreams are made on	55
9	Can Reardon rule again?	62
10	Wales: factory of champions	67
11	Dennis Taylor – laughing all the way to the bank	73
12	Timing: the key to better snooker	76
13	I will survive	79
14	Women's world of snooker	86
15	Snooker stars	95
16	The teenage revolution	101
17	Tony's Australian dream	105
18	Don't shoot the referee	110
19	Why Steve Davis?	115
20	On the road	119
21	The amateur scene	123

Preface

Last year's *World Snooker* was published just before the Embassy World Professional Snooker Championship began. By the time the last ball had been potted in that championship, it was clear that a new *World Snooker* would be required for 1982. There were two main reasons for this. First, and obviously most gratifying to the people connected with the book, was the response from the public. There was an immediate and favourable reaction to a book about snooker which did not try to stun with statistics or lecture on how to play, but instead tried to show something of snooker generally, what it is like to play it, work at it, live it. The other reason, no less gratifying, is that the game continues to expand and develop at a remarkable pace. Almost every month produces a new star, amateur or professional, or a new achievement from *the* player of 1981–2, Steve Davis. Much of this was predictable. Indeed, in the first *World Snooker* we predicted some of it – the growing ascendancy of Steve Davis, the rise of the younger stars, the increasing flow of big money into the game.

In the space of a year exciting new players have come to the top of the professional game. Others have fallen from their position of grace. Yet more wait in the hope that this will be their year. Nothing stands still; no one is safe. The influence of television continues to dominate, prize money and fees exceed one million pounds a year. Some players thrive on the new pressures, others give way to the strain. And over it all stands the record of Steve Davis, beckoning, forcing all players to ever-higher standards.

In *World Snooker No. 2* we try to keep pace with the fast-changing world of snooker, to present some of the stars of today and tomorrow, to discuss the trends and the background to the game, to give a taste of what it is like – being there. Once again the aim has been to give a wide-ranging view of many players, many aspects, without claiming to be comprehensive. Difficult as it is to present the snooker world of today, who can say what the future holds? It is fascinating to speculate, dangerous to predict. It can certainly be said that the public's interest in and knowledge of snooker has increased immeasurably in the last few years and with this informed support the game will continue to maintain a strong position, come what may. If *World Snooker* helps to increase that appreciation and enjoyment, it will have played its part.

Opposite, clockwise from top left: Ray Reardon; Kirk Stevens; Cliff Thorburn; Steve Davis; Tony Meo. Photos: Dave Muscroft.

1

My Crucible view

'Why don't you belt up?' That was all that was said in one of the letters I received from viewers during the 1981 Embassy World Championship. Luckily for me, it wasn't a typical reaction, but it does sometimes set me back a bit to receive such a letter. There is compensation in the rest of the mail – which can be over a hundred letters addressed to me, and each of my fellow commentators receives a similar number – when someone sends in a really appreciative letter saying 'I was so pleased you mentioned such-and-such' or 'Thank you for explaining that point in that way'.

This response from the public is all part of the action at the Crucible, action which occupies most of our waking hours and all of our thoughts for three weeks every year. I enjoy the atmosphere tremendously, the fact that I'm amongst all the best players in the world, that I'm sitting in the best seat in the Arena for this super show . . . it's a very good feeling. It's difficult to describe, but to me it's a feeling of complete enjoyment.

Apart from being in the box and describing the action, I think that the thing I most look forward to is breakfast back at the hotel. Not that I'm obsessive about food – the hours we work in snooker at any level are hardly conducive to being a gourmet – but breakfast time each day is the time when we can sit down and have a long relaxed chat about the events going on around us. The commentators all stay at the same hotel, and when we return at night after a long session we take perhaps half an hour just to relax and then it's off to bed. In the morning it's still inside us, all the excitement and activity – what's going to happen today? Usually there are four or five of us around the table and we discuss the matches we've seen and the ones that have yet to come. We go through all the newspapers debating what each has said. There's a lovely feeling of comradeship and we end up sitting there drinking coffee until it's coming out of our ears! Other meals are fitted in whenever we can get them, so breakfast is really 'our' time of the day.

At the beginning of the championship we have a meeting with the producer, Nick Hunter, who decides the rota we will work. He tries to arrange it so that we are always doing fresh matches in each session rather than keeping with one game throughout. Sometimes we stay with one game if it is very interesting, but generally it works out that the television public gets a different perspective on the same match by listening to different commentators. For example, Ted Lowe will say totally different things from me about Terry Griffiths or Cliff Thorburn, so the commentary keeps fresh all the time. It can be easy to fall into a repetitive rut. That's the hard thing about commentary – describing a fairly restricted field of activity in so many various ways. We all see the game in different ways, from a different viewpoint. For instance, I might think that the player should be going for a snooker but John Pulman, who might be my colleague in the box that day, may think, 'Oh no, he must go for a pot.' We're only trying to read the game: we can't get inside the player's head.

Enjoyable as it all is, it's absolutely exhausting too. At the end of a long session I feel just as worn out as I ever do when I'm playing in a match myself. Instead of just playing my own shots, I'm 'playing' the shots of both players in the match on which I'm commentating.

I believe I'm completely impartial. When I go to Sheffield at the start of the championship I couldn't care – and I don't mean this in any disparaging way – whether Steve Davis or Ray Reardon or Jimmy White wins it. In this years' championship I came in for a bit of criticism because in my commentaries I called Steve Davis 'Stevie'. In fact this prompted one snooker magazine to ask, 'If Jack Karnehm keeps calling Steve Davis "Stevie", why doesn't he call Cliff Thorburn "Cliffie"?' But there wasn't any bias on my part. I suppose that because I've had a little association with Steve as a lad there's some affection there and 'Stevie' is my way of showing that I like him – to me he's a lovely lad. But I also like and respect Cliff Thorburn.

When people criticize players, and every player comes in for criticism, I have to recognize that there must be people who hate the sight of Steve Davis. But there are many who like him. No one ever knows why a particular player arouses strong feelings. There is one player, for example, who I think is colourless, lacking in any very strong features, in fact, as someone once said, 'with all the personality of a slug', and yet that retiring wallflower of a man raises very passionate antipathy. Steve, however, has handled himself well in presenting his personality. In his first television interview with David Vine I thought he was a little brash, rather too full of himself. I saw it as the exuberance of youth; others thought he was just a big-head. But the good thing was that in his next two or three interviews it was very noticeable that he had toned it down. Perhaps someone had whispered in his ear and he had taken heed. After all, at twenty-three he's still only a kid and if he couldn't feel exuberance at his age and in his position, when could he? I think he's beginning to mature into a really fine character.

When I settled down to study the draw I did what every snooker fan does: I tried to forecast who I thought would do well. Of course I had publicly tipped Steve Davis to win. Not a difficult choice to make, considering his form since the previous October when he won the Coral UK Championship. With hindsight I would say that from about the middle of the championship Doug Mountjoy was very much a potential finalist. He was, I think, the most consistent maker of big breaks during the competition, and that is always a reliable guide. His reward for that sort of high consistency was his delightful break of 145 against Ray Reardon which set a new world championship record and earned him a bonus of £6,200. However, to be honest I didn't pick him. I would always rate Doug; I don't

Ray Reardon. Photo: Dave Muscroft.

think I'd back him to win a major championship but I always think he's a jolly good each-way bet. I don't say that with any disrespect, because Doug Mountjoy is a superb player. But in my opinion he's not a great tactician. He's a first-class breakmaker

Below left: Doug Mountjoy.
Below right: Cliff Thorburn. Photos: Dave Muscroft.

WORLD SNOOKER WITH JACK KARNEHM

The stage is set for the final of the 1981 Embassy World Championship at the Crucible Theatre.

when he gets going and he has tremendous courage. He really goes for his game. It's because of that, because he attacks his shots so confidently, that I think he's slightly suspect on his planning – if he misses he leaves his opponent too many chances. At the end of the day he did come through to the final and that was a very fine achievement in which he can well take pride.

In picking my possible semi-finalists I naturally chose Steve Davis. To me, Cliff Thorburn was the other most obvious semi-finalist – and the biggest threat to Steve's chance of taking the title. I had a sneaky feeling somewhere along the line that Tony Meo could do it. He's a very good young player and he has other things going for him. It would be nice for Tony to succeed because his image would bring credit to the game. He projects a wholesome, clean-cut personality, he's not outrageous in his life style: he'd make a very good champion.

Kirk Stevens was next on my short list. I didn't expect him to win, but I thought he could do very well. He's the sort of player, like Alex Higgins, who seems to get in and pot everything. If that sort of player shows good form they can knock their opponents off their game and that's the kind of thing Kirk can do. If he had beaten Dennis Taylor (which he very nearly did), his next match would have been against Doug Mountjoy and who can say how that would have worked out? Two very similar players, both on form – it would have been a real feast of attacking snooker.

I couldn't choose Ray Reardon as a possible semi-finalist. He's been a great champion in the past but I think he has lost confidence. He still has all that talent but when I watch him play I feel that although it's all there, inside him, he hasn't quite got that old confidence to bring it out.

In tipping Tony Meo I was reckoning that he would beat Terry Griffiths. I didn't pick Terry because I take all sorts of things into account, not just ability. I think psychology is coming into the game much more. Players are more aware that they're playing the game 'off the table' – in the bars, in the rest rooms, and so on. I didn't think Terry would handle that aspect quite so well in this year's championship. The increased psychological pressures are shown in a trend I noticed this year much more than in the past: the players now tend not to hang around the Crucible chatting and watching each other's matches. They want to defend themselves that little bit more. To get away from the tensions and perhaps to avoid the possibility of 'psyching' remarks from various people they cleared off out of it as much as they could. In past years the players' box would be full, but this year, if they were still in contention, they watched it privately on television or tucked away in a quiet corner of the theatre. It shows that they're becoming more professional, more independent of each other. With all the money now at stake they can't afford the same old matiness that existed when there were only a dozen or so professionals. It's bound to become more and more a game of conflict and aggression. The players must develop their own defensive mechanisms. Of course they still socialize with each other when the match is over or when they're out of the running, but while the heat of battle is about them they must do what is best for them to keep their psychological 'cool'. If that means hiding in a broom cupboard and standing on their head for two hours (not that anyone I know does so), that is what they must do.

Kirk Stevens. Photo: Dave Muscroft.

An innovation this year was the 'Question Time' we held on television during the breaks in play. I think this is an aspect of the championship that will be given more emphasis in the future. It's terribly important for the game itself that its massive public can write in and have four or five experts answering their questions or explaining some part of the game in greater depth. After all, commentary is about

MY CRUCIBLE VIEW

saying what you see, and while you're describing what you see you cannot explain things as fully as you might wish.

From the enormous bundles of mail that come into the Crucible we are made very aware that there is a vast audience out there, watching avidly and noting carefully everything we say. The idea that sixteen million people are looking in and listening to me doesn't worry me. Everything we say in the commentary box is recorded and we have the 'safety net' that if we say something naughty we know that it can be cut before the programme is shown. Not that anyone says anything very bad – which is just as well, because the cost of editing the video tape is quite high.

Quite a few people have asked me about Tony Meo's extremely short stint in the commentary box during the 1981 championship. The producers like to bring the players into the box for it adds a little interest and the public likes to hear their comments. Tony came in, and after making a few comments we saw a really fine shot. Tony said, 'My God, that was a beautiful shot,' then for the rest of the session not another word was heard from him. Some viewers were under the impression that Nick Hunter had thrown a lasso into the box and pulled Tony out by the neck for this indiscretion, but in fact what happened was not nearly so dramatic: Tony had suddenly realized that playing snooker isn't quite the same as sitting in the commentary box talking about it, and he just dried up. He was prompted a couple of times but couldn't get anything out.

Doing a commentary isn't as easy as it may seem. The only time the thought of the audience affects me is when we go 'live'. We know in advance that a particular session will be live, so we are not suddenly thrown in at the deep end. When the commentary is live, the sensation coming through my headphones is different. For some technical reason, it is a peculiar hollow feeling – as if I'm going out to the whole world. It really is an electric experience, tremendously exciting. I find that when this happens I become even more involved in the game than usual and my feeling for the players is heightened. If it is a close game, the excitement is in every shot. No one can project excitement if there's nothing interesting happening, but the additional 'buzz' I experience at these times shows that I'm not entirely unaffected by live broadcasting.

As the championship plays through and the second table in the arena is removed to concentrate all attention on one table, some of my predictions have fallen by the wayside. We can see that one of the four remaining gladiators will be the next world champion. I believe that it is very important for the

Photo: Dave Muscroft.

Alex Higgins is watched closely by his opponent Steve Davis in the second round of the 1981 Embassy World Championship.

game that we should have the right sort of champion. There may be half a million players in the world, especially the younger ones, who will follow the example set by him. Look at players like Jimmy White, Kirk Stevens and Terry Whitthread, for example – who can doubt that they were influenced by the style of Alex Higgins? When Alex won in 1972 all the kids decided that the best way to play the game was to belt around the table and jump up in the air while hitting the ball. That works for Alex, but there's only one Alex Higgins. He's the only one who can crash about playing these fantastic flamboyant shots. What his imitators don't perhaps realize is that there is a lot of science in Alex's game. He's a very knowledgeable player – look at the close attention he pays to the selection of cues – and even if he's not one to discuss the whys and wherefores of his methods he knows exactly what he's trying to do.

My point is that if all the young players in the country try to emulate Alex Higgins, I'm afraid that we will have a whole generation of players copying all the wrong things – things that Alex can do but they can't. Ray Reardon was an excellent champion from the point of view of setting an example. He wasn't a 'flash' young man like Alex, and therefore perhaps his influence on play wasn't quite so obvious, yet his example was paramount in setting an image for the game, a responsible professional image which brought snooker into the modern age. Terry Griffiths and Cliff Thorburn also made their contributions as champion – not least because they are personable young men and they increased the ladies' interest in snooker. Cliff's success, of course, also gave a great boost to the game in Canada. I believe that if Doug Mountjoy had won the title in 1981 he would have been a champion in the same mould as Reardon. The youngsters would have followed his style to some extent and he would have been a fine champion.

However, the thing that excites me, especially in my capacity as National Coach in England, is the potential of Steve Davis's example as champion. He has the right image to attract the younger generation – and there may be half a million youngsters who will copy the Steve Davis style. I cannot disguise my admiration for his game. He is virtually the perfect text-book example of a player. When we talk about this concept of 'image' it is important to remember that what is copied first and foremost is the visual image. In Steve we have a young man who is unquestionably as fabulous in his own way as Alex is in his. If I had to choose between Steve and Alex in terms of what is better for the younger players to follow, I would have to choose Steve. He has the sound technique, the discipline, the correct attitude to the game. Perhaps it's also fair to say that in watching Steve the youngsters can see what he's doing. So often when Alex plays a great shot we can only wonder, 'How did he do that?' If all young players set out to copy Steve, knowing from what they have read in the newspapers and seen on television that dedication and hard work play an important part in success, I really believe that this will develop the game and raise the general standard of play. It will probably produce a champion of the future and I find this a very exciting prospect.

Of course, we're not going to have half a million Steve Davis clones. We wouldn't want that. Each player will develop in their own manner, interpreting Steve's game in a way personal to him or her. The lesson will be adjusted according to each player's character: that is what the game is all about. It won't stop with Steve Davis. Other champions will come along with different methods and they will add further dimensions to the game. Steve has God's gift of a sweet cue action and many of his followers will never achieve that. It's not all done by practice and hard work, although these help. It is a gift.

In my view there are going to be many more youngsters like Steve Davis, Jimmy White and Tony Meo on the scene. The younger people are seeing more and better snooker, they're getting more opportunity to play the game in the increasing number of snooker clubs and leisure centres, and there's a lot more effective coaching available to them. I wonder, as we look forward to future championships, if the established players of today, the thirty-five- and forty-year-olds, are soon going to be made into the old men of the game by all these fine young players coming up. It must worry them. The up-and-coming kids are like terriers snapping at their ankles – no matter how you beat them down or shoo them away, they keep coming back. I wouldn't be surprised if, in five years time, the majority of the players at the Crucible are under twenty-five years old. The frightening thing about successful young players like Jimmy White is that not only are they very good but they also seem to be so *seasoned* at such a ridiculously early age. They're beginning to out-general the older players.

The average age of the top stars has lowered incredibly in the last few years. It's not a fluke. The old theory was that if you were one of the top seeds, you were kept away from the 'snarling pack' until you were at the very final stages which were held over enormously long distances. It wasn't so very long ago that the final match alone took two weeks to play – something like best of 141 frames! Some twelve years ago, when I was chairman of the Billiards Association and Control Council (now the B & SCC), I suggested that the final should be played over 45 frames. Some of the players were quite horrified at the thought of this 'short sprint' distance. The older players preferred the longer games because they gave them time to settle into a rhythm which suited their style. Nowadays the matches are quite short and the older style of player can be easily bustled out of his stride by a young player coming in and potting everything in sight. The reduced length of matches is a big factor in the rise of youth.

In the few quiet reflective moments at the Crucible, when the crowds have gone home, the table has been covered and only a lonely cleaner occupies the centre of the snooker world's stage, it is difficult not to ponder on the many changes the game has seen in a few short years and to consider its future.

The Crucible's position as the centre of the game has been the subject of much speculation. There are many who believe it is too small to accommodate all the spectators who clamour to obtain seats. This is certainly true, as hundreds of ticket applications are returned each year and the queues around the theatre grow ever longer. I appreciate that point of view, but personally I feel – having lived through fifty years of billiards and snooker, having seen the game flourish, then die and stay dead for over ten years before reviving to prosper as never before – that the Crucible is now accepted as the one place that cannot be topped. No one would move the FA Cup Final from Wembley or the All-England Tennis from Wimbledon. Would a Cup Final held in Catford have the same appeal? I think that there are terrible risks in moving from this virtually ideal setting to an untried and unknown location. In any event, I believe that the perfect snooker audience should not exceed one thousand or so. Above that figure some of the atmosphere and intimacy is lost. While I sympathize with the people who cannot obtain tickets, I think that the good of the game is paramount and I don't think we should interfere with a successful formula. I dread the thought of a theatre twice the size of the Crucible which may be only half-full in the first week. The newspapers might report, 'The place is half-empty, snooker has lost its appeal.' Knowing the power of the press and the media, I fear the sort of chain reaction that such reports might cause.

Another theatre would hold only about six hundred more people per session. Compared with the sixteen million who watch on television, that is not a large number. Television has made this game what it is today and I feel that it is very much in the game's interest to retain its television audience rather than to increase facilities for only a slightly larger number of committed fans. Television has shown the world that snooker is an intelligent, attractive game equal to or better than tennis or golf. Ticket-buying spectators in numbers beyond our wildest dreams would still not compare with the most modest television audience. Let us not forget that we do not face the position that American boxing once reached, where the fights were held only for the convenience of the cameras and the audience was virtually redundant. I don't think we ever will reach that position. The audience in the Crucible is a genuine audience who have paid real money to see real matches. Let us not forget, too, that in the pre-television days, in the best 'good old days' the game ever had, they never had such a large audience at Burroughes and Watts or the Royal Horticultural Hall as are now taken for granted at the Crucible. I realize that the game must grow and develop and some of the changes will not meet with my approval but, speaking for myself, I hope that I'll be returning to my seat in the commentary box in the Crucible Theatre, the best seat in snooker, for many years to come!

Tony Meo. Photo: Dave Muscroft.

Terry Griffiths. Photo: Dave Muscroft.

World Snooker with Jack Karnehm

Results of the Embassy World Championship 1981

QUALIFYING ROUNDS

Played at Redwood Lodge Country Club, Bristol

Tony Knowles (Bolton)	7	Chris Ross (Woking)	0
		(Ross retired at the end of the 7th frame)	
Tony Knowles	9	Jim Wych (Calgary)	3
Cliff Wilson (Caldicot)	9	Roy Andrewartha (Wallasey)	4
Eddie Sinclair (Glasgow)	9	Paddy Morgan (Australia)	8
Cliff Wilson	9	Eddie Sinclair	8
John Dunning (Yorkshire)	9	Bernard Bennett (Southampton)	6
John Dunning	9	Patsy Fagan (London)	8
Dave Martin (Co. Durham)	9	Ian Anderson (Australia)	3
Dave Martin	9	John Pulman (London)	2

Tony Knowles, Cliff Wilson, John Dunning and Dave Martin therefore qualified for the competition proper.

Played at Romiley Forum, Stockport

Tony Meo (London)	9	Joe Johnson (Bradford)	8
Mike Hallett (Grimsby)	9	Frank Jonik (Toronto)	1
Tony Meo	9	Mike Hallett	4
Jimmy White (London)	9	Bernie Mikkelsen (Toronto)	4
Jimmy White	9	Jimmy Meadowcroft (Lancs)	8
Willie Thorne (Leicester)	9	Marrio Morra (Toronto)	5
David Greaves (Blackpool)	9	Maurice Parkin (Yorkshire)	5
Willie Thorne	9	David Greaves	3
Ray Edmonds (Grimsby)	9	Mark Wildman (Peterborough)	3
Rex Williams (Stourbridge)	9	Sid Hood (Grimsby)	4
Ray Edmonds	9	Rex Williams	7

Tony Meo, Jimmy White, Willie Thorne and Ray Edmonds therefore qualified for the competition proper.

COMPETITION PROPER

Played at the Crucible Theatre, Sheffield

First Round

Graham Miles (Birmingham)	10	Tony Knowles	8
David Taylor (Manchester)	10	Cliff Wilson	6
Tony Meo	10	John Virgo (Northampton)	6
Steve Davis (London)	10	Jimmy White	8
Doug Mountjoy (Ebbw Vale)	10	Willie Thorne	6
Kirk Stevens (Toronto)	10	John Dunning	4
Bill Werbeniuk (Vancouver)	10	Dave Martin	4
John Spencer (Bolton)	10	Ray Edmonds	9

MY CRUCIBLE VIEW

Second Round

Cliff Thorburn (Toronto)	13	Graham Miles	2
David Taylor	13	Fred Davis (Stourport)	3
Terry Griffiths (Llanelli)	13	Tony Meo	6
Steve Davis	13	Alex Higgins (Manchester)	8
Doug Mountjoy	13	Eddie Charlton (Australia)	7
Dennis Taylor (Blackburn)	13	Kirk Stevens	11
Bill Werbeniuk	13	Pierrie Mans (South Africa)	5
Ray Reardon (Stoke)	13	John Spencer	11

Quarter-finals

Ray Reardon	13	Bill Werbeniuk	10
Doug Mountjoy	13	Dennis Taylor	8
Cliff Thorburn	13	David Taylor	6
Steve Davis	13	Terry Griffiths	9

Semi-finals

Doug Mountjoy	16	Ray Reardon	10
Steve Davis	16	Cliff Thorburn	10

Before and after. Referee John Williams is flanked by 1981 World Championship finalists Doug Mountjoy (left) and Steve Davis; the inset picture shows a victorious Steve. Photos: Dave Muscroft.

FINAL

Steve Davis	18
Doug Mountjoy	12

The Supreme Snooker League

The official ratings list of the world's top thirty-two players (see opposite) has been criticized because it takes account of the players' performances in the Embassy World Championship only and it 'stores up' these performances over a period of three years. If status is judged on results of two or three years ago, the list cannot accurately reflect the current scene, and of course as the official list rests on only one championship it follows that if an otherwise successful player has an 'off' day on the wrong day his place in the official ratings will not be a true reflection of his current form or ability.

Is there a fairer way of doing it? Probably, although neither we nor the governing body of the professional game have yet devised it. Is there another way of rating the players which would take account of their performances in other tournaments and be up to date, applying only to the current year? There is – although it must be said that the list put forward in this chapter (see page 19) is every bit as unfair and inconsistent as the official ratings list. In some cases it is wickedly capricious, but it disregards reputation, status, publicity and any results of the past. It must be remembered that a comprehensive list, balanced to satisfy a statistician, is almost impossible to collate because many of snooker's major tournaments are by invitation only and players, no matter how good they are, can make no impression in a tournament in which they are unable to compete. In addition, even the most respectable and serious championships have built-in exemptions for the top seeded players so that, for example, a top-eight player would have to play only four matches to win a major title while the lower-rated professionals would have to play anything up to nine games to win first prize. So the system is 'loaded' in favour of the better player. The performance chart clearly disapproves of the exemptions system and, fed only on results, shows its inclination to anarchy and in fact 'loads' in favour of the lesser players.

The list analyses the performances of all the players on those occasions when they were able to compete and some interesting results emerge. It is, no doubt, a grave disadvantage to an ambitious player not to be invited into every tournament, but the chart sympathizes with this and records better results on the basis that if a man isn't in too many tournaments he can't be beaten too often. The list is based on the following tournaments held in 1980–1: Champion of Champions (London 1980), Coral UK Championship (Preston 1980), Benson & Hedges (London 1981), Benson & Hedges (Dublin 1981), Yamaha International (Derby 1981), Embassy World Championship (Sheffield 1981), Jameson Open (Derby 1981). In addition, the national championships of England and Wales are included, but the Irish title is not as it was played on a challenge basis between holder Dennis Taylor and Patsy Fagan. The Scottish Professional Championship is still in its infancy and, with apologies to Scotland, it is left out of account in this chart.

Willie Thorne. Photo: Dave Muscroft.

THE SUPREME SNOOKER LEAGUE

WPBSA Ratings List 1980–1

		POINTS 1978	1979	1980	Total
1	Ray Reardon	5	2	2	9
2	Cliff Thorburn	2	1	5	8
3	Eddie Charlton	3	3	2	8
4	Alex Higgins	1	2	4	7
5	Terry Griffiths	-	5	1	6
6	Dennis Taylor	1	4	1	6
7	Pierrie Mans	4	1	1	6
8	Fred Davis	3	2	1	6
9	David Taylor	1	1	3	5
10	Bill Werbeniuk	2	2	1	5
11	Kirk Stevens	-	1	3	4
12	John Virgo	0	3	1	4
13	Steve Davis	-	1	2	3
14	Doug Mountjoy	1	1	1	3
15	John Spencer	1	1	1	3
16	Graham Miles	2	1	0	3
17	Jim Wych	-	0	2	2
18	Patsy Fagan	2	0	0	2
19	Willie Thorne	1	0	0	1
20	John Pulman	1	0	0	1
21	Pat Houlihan	1	0	0	1

Jimmy White. Photo: Dave Muscroft.

WPBSA Ratings List 1981–2

		POINTS 1979	1980	1981	Total
1	Cliff Thorburn	1	5	3	9
2	Steve Davis	1	2	5	8
3	Terry Griffiths	5	1	2	8
4	Ray Reardon	2	2	3	7
5	Dennis Taylor	4	1	2	7
6	Doug Mountjoy	1	1	4	6
7	David Taylor	1	3	2	6
8	Eddie Charlton	3	2	1	6
9	Bill Werbeniuk	2	1	2	5
10	Kirk Stevens	1	3	1	5
11	Alex Higgins	2	4	1 (-2)	5
12	Fred Davis	2	1	1	4
13	John Virgo	3	1	0	4
14	John Spencer	1	1	1	3
15	Pierrie Mans	1	1	1	3
16	Graham Miles	1	0	1	2
17	Jim Wych	0	2	0	2
18	Tony Meo	-	0	1	1
19	Ray Edmonds				
20	Tony Knowles				
21	Jimmy White				
22	Willie Thorne				
23	Cliff Wilson				
24	Dave Martin				
25	John Dunning				
26	Jim Meadowcroft				
27	Patsy Fagan				
28	Rex Williams				
29	Mike Hallett				
30	Eddie Sinclair				
31	David Greaves				
32	John Pulman				

As with everything else in professional snooker in 1981, Steve Davis comes first. But look at the margin of his ascendancy: in frames played he holds a slightly better than 2-1 lead over all opposition. He is of course the most successful professional of the year, and in getting to the final match of each of his tournaments he has recorded more frames played than anyone else – 118 more frames than the next most active professional, Ray Reardon, to be precise. The list is in fact unique because it shows a larger number of frames played by Steve than he can ever achieve again, even with the same success, unless tournaments are to be played monthly. His high figures are partly due to the fact that in the early part of the record he had to enter tournaments at an earlier stage than the 'big boys' and

John Spencer. Photo: Dave Muscroft.

David Taylor. Photo: Dave Muscroft.

Dave Martin. Photo: Dave Muscroft.

accordingly played more frames in reaching the final of the Coral UK or the Embassy World Championships. Even if Ray Reardon or Cliff Thorburn had enjoyed all Steve's successes, they could not have matched his colossal number of frames played because they entered the events at later stages.

Remembering that in studying the list we must disregard reputation and those events in which a player did not compete, Willie Thorne is not such a surprise in second place. He is one of the finest players in England, a man who tends to lose – often unluckily – by the narrowest of margins. This shows up in his percentage rate. No one scores 9-0 or 9-1 wins over Willie Thorne, and if a few of his close defeats had been close victories there is no telling how far he might have gone in this year.

Doug Mountjoy, with a good run in the Embassy World Championship, losing in the final, comes out with third place. Despite the illness that troubled him in the early part of the year, he is clearly the most successful (after Steve Davis) of those players who were able to compete in everything that was going. This gives added value to his high placing. He was also one of the few players actually to win a big event – the Champion of Champions in London.

Patsy Fagan in fourth place appears to be something of a 'freak' result, but again it reflects his very narrow defeats in the few events in which he was able to take part.

The next most successful of those leading men who were a feature of most tournaments is Terry Griffiths. He too is a winner – of the Irish Benson & Hedges (and of the Pontin Professional too, though it is not counted in this chart). His play has been consistent throughout the year, although he has not regularly shown his world-beating form of 1979.

In sixth position the list shows its merits in being able to rate a very promising newcomer more accurately and quickly than the official list could. Tony Meo played a substantial number of big tournament frames, was not in the 'invitation' events, but nevertheless scored an impressive success rate over 221 frames.

The Welsh team of 'top achievers' is completed by Ray Reardon entering the list at seventh place. Apart from Steve Davis, the leading men who were in most tournaments, maintained a high success rate *and* won something were all Welsh. Ray's win was the Woodpecker Welsh Professional Championship – not even Steve Davis could win that!

Again, in eighth position the list gives justice and proper credit to a man who has slipped out of the official list but who, in the last year, has mounted the most impressive 'comeback' of the modern game. He has performed superbly to come through from tough qualifying groups to reclaim his place in the top levels of snooker: Rex Williams, former World Professional Billiards Champion and no mean snooker player, had been written off as a top contender. His business interests and his career in television commentary clearly affected his form in the late seventies, but he has re-dedicated himself to the game and beaten many of the 'young hopefuls' to show that he must still be taken seriously. He was himself a 'boy wonder' once the youngest-ever professional player. He was written off too soon. The message from this chart is clear: Rex Williams is back.

David Taylor of Manchester, a player who has improved and developed his game almost in exact synchronization with the rise of snooker itself, earns a place in this top ten as he does in the official one. He has shown tremendous fighting qualities and skills to establish himself as the sort of player who will now only be beaten by the best if they are at their best. A good year for him – and a well-deserved success rate.

John Spencer may not win the big tournaments the way he used to, but his record in this year shows that he is still very much in the picture. His position also reflects some very close defeats and there were a number of very good players among his victories.

Eddie Sinclair of Scotland, with only one appearance (in the Coral UK) benefits from the chart's logic (or lack of it) to take eleventh place – but he did lose by only one frame and consequently his percentage is high.

Alex Higgins in twelfth place? It's not so far from his official rating of eleven and perhaps it reflects the erratic course his victories and defeats can take. He has taken part in as many matches as Terry Griffiths, been where the bullets fly, and has still scored over 50 per cent. He is also one of the few winners – in the London Benson & Hedges – and was a close and rather unlucky loser to Steve Davis in the Jameson Open semi-final.

The last of the players with a tournament record better than 50 per cent is Dennis Taylor of Northern Ireland. His official rating makes him one of the players invited to take part in nearly every significant event and he joins the other five players in the top section of this chart who have been exposed to the fiercest competition and survived it with a good percentage rate.

The list again shows its flexibility and immediacy by placing Dave Martin in fourteenth position. He qualified for the Embassy World Championship and, starting in the qualifying groups, reached the semi-final of the Jameson Open – a great achievement for a new professional and the chart confirms his status as one of the players who made an impression this season.

Canadian Bill Werbeniuk played quite consistently as always, but lost crucial matches that could have taken him much further. He has 'cured' the shake in his cueing arm by drinking many pints of lager while playing (his major victory in 1981 came when the Inland Revenue accepted his contention that this was the only way to control his cueing arm and allowed all the lager as a tax deduction!). No matter what sort of list was devised, Bill would always be there or thereabouts in the top fifteen, but the feeling persists that he could do better.

The next three places are taken by the fairly new professionals, Cliff Wilson, Ray Edmonds and Tony Knowles, starting to establish themselves firmly on the tournament circuit. Each of them still needs that big break to get through to the upper reaches of the game, but our chart reflects a quite successful year and there are prospects of much more to come from all three.

At nineteenth place the list bares its claws and shows what can happen to a top star who competes in everything but loses too many matches. Cliff Thorburn of Canada, rated official number one in the world, has had an unhappy year in the big events and suffers the ignominy of a lowly place. It is interesting to note that one of his most surprising defeats of the year, 5-0 to Graham Miles in the Jameson Open, of itself cost him three or four places on the list. Graham Miles, with some better performances this year than in any of the last three, shows up at twentieth place.

The next six places are taken by new or fairly new

Cliff Wilson. Photo: Dave Muscroft.

Ray Edmonds. Photo: Dave Muscroft.
Inset: Eddie gets ready. Photo: Dave Muscroft.

professionals, with the exception of the experienced John Virgo at twenty-third place. He has not had a good year, and a few severe losses, especially at the hands of Tony Meo, give him this unaccustomed low rating. On ability he should be somewhere in the top ten – but the chart is merciless, only results count.

Once again, in twenty-eighth place, the list metes out punishment to a player who was in nearly every tournament but did not do very well in any of them, and again it is a Canadian who suffers. Kirk Stevens, officially rated tenth in the world, felt the full blast of exposure to top tournaments when he was unable to produce his best form. In the end the chart shows that he 'lost' by an overall 2-1 frames margin and he knows where the bullets fly because a large number of them hit him! Like many of the players in the lower reaches of this list, Kirk had a very busy and rewarding season on the exhibition circuit but to someone like Kirk, who is desperately anxious to produce his best in tournament play, this is little consolation.

Fred Davis, not as active as he once was and meeting too many strong players, appears in twenty-ninth position. Possibly the list is exercising another of its many powers in reflecting that in modern snooker there is little respect for age when winning counts! This is the lowest rating of any kind ever given to Fred in his life – but he is still very high in the popularity polls.

THE SUPREME SNOOKER LEAGUE

The last of the big names to fall into the basement of the list is Eddie Charlton of Australia. His year in England has been little short of disastrous. He competed in three tournaments, the Embassy World Championship, the London Benson & Hedges and the Jameson Open, and was knocked out in his first match in all three events. This gave him his most unsuccessful year in England since he first started playing in tournaments in 1968.

Who then are the best thirty-two players in the world in 1981–2? This list does not claim to give the answer; it merely records what actually happened when the famous and the not-so-famous were called upon to show what they could do against their fellow professionals. But the official WPBSA list, based on only *one* championship over three years, does claim to answer the question. Is it more accurate? Is it fairer? The leading professionals (as they are generally understood to be) will certainly think so. They may be right. We make no claims for this chart except to suggest that it is probably more interesting than the official list – and certainly more volatile.

The Supreme Snooker League Table

		MATCHES PLAYED	FRAMES PLAYED	FRAMES WON	FRAMES LOST	PERCENTAGE FRAMES WON
1	Steve Davis	29	352	235	117	66.76
2	Willie Thorne	6	78	48	30	61.54
3	Doug Mountjoy	19	220	126	94	57.27
4	Patsy Fagan	4	45	25	20	55.56
5	Terry Griffiths	21	217	118	99	54.38
6	Tony Meo	11	144	77	67	53.47
7	Ray Reardon	20	234	125	109	53.42
8	Rex Williams	6	62	33	29	53.23
9	David Taylor	7	95	50	45	52.63
10	John Spencer	11	130	68	62	52.31
11	Eddie Sinclair	2	29	15	14	51.72
12	Alex Higgins	21	223	115	108	51.57
13	Dennis Taylor	18	167	86	81	51.50
14	Dave Martin	6	51	25	26	49.02
15	Bill Werbeniuk	8	83	40	43	48.19
16	Cliff Wilson	4	57	27	30	47.37
17	Ray Edmonds	9	83	39	44	46.99
18	Tony Knowles	3	32	15	17	46.88
19	Cliff Thorburn	15	142	66	76	46.48
20	Graham Miles	15	132	61	71	46.21
21	Roy Andrewartha	3	38	17	21	44.74
22	Jimmy White	4	27	12	15	44.44
23	John Virgo	15	133	58	75	43.61
24	Pierrie Mans	5	51	22	29	43.14
25	Joe Johnson	4	42	17	25	40.48
25	Mark Wildman	3	42	17	25	40.48
27	John Pulman	1	15	6	9	40.00
28	Kirk Stevens	12	106	41	65	38.68
29	Fred Davis	10	91	34	57	37.36
30	John Dunning	3	40	13	27	32.50
31	Mike Hallett	4	19	6	13	31.58
32	Eddie Charlton	3	32	9	23	28.13

3

What the heck do they mean?

Billiards and snooker are very technical games. Fortunately for us all, it is possible to watch and appreciate snooker without being able to play it. It is also possible to explain and commentate on what is happening on the table without going into intensely detailed discussion. I think we're lucky that the technical terms of the game – the language of the billiard table – are not too numerous and therefore anyone can tune in the television set and have a reasonable understanding of what is going on.

There are, however, some technical terms which may not be self-explanatory and it would perhaps be useful to discuss these. Part of our job in the commentary box is to keep things clear and simple, but it may be that we use a particular term and, because of the state of play, we do not have time to explain it. The most usual terms are discussed in this chapter, and after a study of these I hope you won't find yourself saying 'What the heck do they mean?' next time you watch a snooker match.

I only wish that all the words and phrases were as graphic and self-explanatory as the favourite phrase of my colleague John Pulman. When John describes a really fine winning performance he is wont to say, 'He did him like a kipper.' He's never had to explain that phrase!

The shot to nothing

This is a very common term, but as I go around the clubs and listen to people I am surprised at the number of times the expression is misused.

Every shot involves a possible advantage to the person who plays it (the striker), and when he is considering what to play he must weigh the 'negative' aspect of the shot, i.e the risk involved if he fails to do what he set out to do. A 'shot to nothing' is one in which the risk to the striker is minimal or non-existent. That is to say, he takes a good positive chance but if he fails to pot the ball he will come back to a position of safety, leaving no risk to himself.

The typical shot to nothing can often be seen in the early stages of the frame. A red may have become detached from the pack. The striker will attempt to cut it into a top pocket (cueing from the baulk end), bringing the cue ball all the way back down the table so that if he has been successful with the pot he can proceed to a minor colour (yellow, green or brown), but if he fails to pot the red the cue ball is left miles away from the reds and gives his opponent little chance to profit from the 'leave'.

It is often possible to play what appears to be a very bold shot which is still a shot to nothing. Let us say that a red is in the area of the 'D', just below the brown, with the cue ball behind it and on line for the middle pocket. To pot the red into the middle a gentle shot will be required, with the possibility that the red may 'stick' on the lip of the pocket. The shot can be played with all the delicacy required and it will look foolhardy – but a little 'stun' on the cue ball will keep it sheltered by the brown and even if the pot is unsuccessful the opponent's way to the enticing red is snookered by the brown. On the other hand, if the pot is successful the brown can be potted into the same pocket and a break built up from there. The colours can often be used to defend the cue ball while you attack a red.

A 'shot to nothing' means, therefore, 'an opportunity offering little or no risk'. It does not mean 'a shot to gain nothing' as some people seem to believe. A shot like that – for example, if there is a red on the edge of the top pocket and no colours around and the player trundles the cue ball into the red to pot it, leaving himself on the edge of the pocket with no position at all – doesn't have a technical term. I have heard it called a 'nothing shot'; I prefer to call it a foolish shot.

The shot to nothing, properly used, is a valuable tactical weapon. Of course, things can go wrong, but if it truly is a shot to nothing (and not just wishful thinking) it gives a great advantage to the striker. I don't think there is a technical term for the opposite of a shot to nothing. That, I would think, is a shot where the risk of failure far outweighs any positive advantage to be gained from playing it. For example, where missing the pot will leave all the reds open and the cue ball nicely placed among them. When such a shot succeeds it is often called a 'do-or-die shot'. When it fails it's called stupid! I would call it one to avoid playing if you possibly can.

WHAT THE HECK DO THEY MEAN?

A double-barrelled shot

This is a shot which has two objectives and not merely the obvious one of, for instance, potting the ball and leaving some sort of position. Usually in snooker it is a shot calculated to pot the object ball and 'cannon' into another to improve its position. The cannon is a basic shot in billiards and to make it is to strike the other two balls with the cue ball. The cannon has tremendous positional and break-building advantages in both games – very often in snooker a player plays to pot and cannon into another ball or balls in the same stroke. The object of the cannon is to improve the position of the cannoned ball, at the same time acting as a check on the pace of the cue ball in a variety of ways depending on the type of contact necessary for positional purposes. All these subtle skills are built into the shot according to the ability of the player involved.

There is a subtle double-barrelled shot played by the best players (although they may deny it) which involves, when the position of the balls demands it, a safety shot with the main objective of getting safe but the additional objective of not getting *too* safe so that the opponent is tempted into having a go at a very difficult pot. This one requires confidence and the knowledge or hope that you're a better player than your opponent.

The kick

The kick is a term used to denote that an unnatural result has occurred from the contact of the shot played. The cue ball and object ball kick apart, very often causing a total breakdown of the shot. This effect can and does have varying effects on a player's confidence.

The reason for this reaction by the balls is not positively ascertained as yet. Players and technical experts have offered various explanations some based on scientific reason, others on more practical grounds. As so often occurs in these situations, some explanations are based on personal likes and dislikes governed by a variety of factors and are not worth discussion. The fact remains that in the World Billiards Championship in London in 1950, when the type of ball used today was not even available, kicks were happening, and also occurred before that time: it is nothing new. It is true, however, that since the introduction of the lighter ball, kicks occur more frequently. In my view the weight factor combined with the general conditions under which we play today cause this phenomenon. The simple explanation is that a foreign body, such as dust or chalk, gets between the two points of contact and creates a bad effect. This can happen when players are careless with chalk and scrub away too much on the tip of the cue, depositing dust on the table which is then picked up by the balls. A kick is more likely to happen when a perfect full-ball contact is made on the object ball, particularly when top is applied to the cue ball. The cue ball can climb the object ball before it parts company with it. The full contact ensures maximum resistance to the cue ball in terms of weight, and also a similar direction of travel for both balls. The top spin has a clinging effect, therefore it should be obvious that the heavier the balls, the less likely will be the lifting of the cue ball in the normal execution of shots.

The nap of the cloth can play its part in causing a kick too if the contact takes place across a deep finger mark made by a moist bridge hand. The cue ball can be standing fractionally higher on the raised nap of the dragged hand mark, whilst the object ball is lower on a smooth part, thus creating conditions in which the climb is more likely to happen. Humidity and heavy nap effects are also leading culprits. It has been suggested that static electricity builds up from time to time and causes a miniature explosion when certain contact is made. I would not doubt that this is possible, as indeed are many of the reasons put forward. However, I am convinced that the reintroduction of the heavier ball would reduce the number of kicks to the level of those days when they were considered merely as unfortunate occurrences rather than an indictment of the manufacturers' ability to produce a good ball.

Baulk line

The line which goes across the table 29 inches from the bottom cushion is called the baulk line. It is important in the rules of billiards but has no significance in the rules of snooker. During the Embassy World Championship in 1981 we had suggestions from television viewers that if it's not needed then it shouldn't be there and snooker should be played on a table which has only the 'D' marked on it. I wouldn't agree with that suggestion. It must be said that even if snooker is the dominant game today, it is still played on a billiard table. Strictly speaking, there is no such thing as a snooker table. While it might suit some people to see the baulk line removed, it would cause a lot of inconvenience in the trade and in clubs if tables had to be re-marked according to whether the players wanted to play billiards or snooker.

Although the baulk line is irrelevant to the rules of snooker its presence on the table does no harm, and let no one tell you that it is irrelevant to the *playing* of snooker. Many players use it as a

The baulk line and 'D' are clearly shown in this shot of Steve Davis opening a frame. Photo: Dave Muscroft.

'landmark' in safety play, especially in escaping from snookers. If it's there, use it: there is nothing in the rules against this.

The baulk end

This is of course the area behind the baulk line, and the 'D' is the semi-circle in the centre of the baulk line (the radius of which is 11½ inches). At the start of the game, or when a player has gone in-off, the cue ball is said to be 'in hand'. The next player is therefore allowed to start his next shot by placing the cue ball anywhere in the 'D'. If he places it outside the 'D' and strikes it, he commits a foul shot.

Top

When a player applies 'top' to the cue ball he strikes it above centre. This causes the cue ball to run further so that when it strikes the object ball it continues its forward motion. Very useful for positional play.

Stun

When a player considers the table prior to taking his shot it is very often the case that the best place for his cue ball to go to after making the pot (and certainly the one from which the next shot can be clearly seen) is the position already occupied by the object ball. The way to achieve this is by the 'stun' shot. Hitting the cue ball slightly below centre with a nice firm action will leave it dead on position. Hit it too high and it will run through (top); hit it too low and it may screw back.

Screw

One of the most attractive shots in snooker, in which the cue ball goes forward to contact the object ball, then comes straight back like a yo-yo on a string. It is not an easy shot to master with precision but it is absolutely essential in top-class snooker. It is achieved by imparting 'back spin' on the cue ball with the cue. The cue must strike low and really push through the cue ball – force is not always necessary.

Half-ball

This is one of the most useful aids to aiming and potting. It describes the position where the cue, correctly addressing the centre of the cue ball, follows a line which runs through the outer edge of the object ball. If the angle is recognized by the player (and it is a very common one) he knows exactly the line of aim to pot the ball. It is an extremely valuable scoring position in billiards (for in-offs) and from a recognition of true half-ball shots the player gives himself a guide to all the other set-piece angles such as quarter-ball and threequarter-ball.

The term 'half-ball', therefore, describes the relationship of two balls to each other and does not indicate that a ball is somehow defective. This is not always true, however, in the case of balls used by Eddie Agha of Montreal, who is one of the world's leading exponents of trick shots. During his exhibitions he invites a young child out of the audience to have a shot at potting a ball. Eddie places the object ball carefully, the child aims and (eventually) hits it. As soon as the object ball is struck it falls apart in two neat halves to the horror of the child and the delight of the audience!

A plant

A plant is the position in which a ball is not potable by direct contact with the cue ball but is potted by the cue ball striking (usually) another red first and causing that red to pot the second red. These shots offer great possibilities for extending breaks when there appear to be no potable reds available. Very often a plant will be lurking on the table – but very often too the player will fail to notice it. Where two reds lie in a direct line to the pocket the plant is obvious, but sometimes the line is not quite so apparent and a bit of thought and careful calculation must go into the shot. It must always be remembered that the success of these shots depends on the first red taking the line that would have been taken by the cue ball in a direct shot. All good players must be able to recognize and use plants when they occur. One of the most noticeable things about the Canadian players is their extensive knowledge and use of this sort of shot.

Touching ball

Where the cue ball is touching a ball 'on' (i.e. one that the striker can lawfully hit), the referee must call 'Touching ball' and must indicate the ball to which he refers. The rule is that if the striker plays his cue ball away from the touching ball without moving it he is deemed to have struck it legitimately and is not required to strike any other ball. If he moves the touching ball it is a push stroke and a foul. For his own protection, therefore, the striker needs to know if it is a touching ball.

In close safety play around the pack of reds (where this position most often occurs) it is a great advantage if the balls are touching rather than, say, 1 millimetre apart. If the balls are not touching, the striker is faced with a very difficult shot in which he must hit something without causing a push stroke or leaving anything for his opponent. However, if he has a touching ball it is relatively simple to judge an excellent safety shot – as he is not required to hit anything – and he can, for example, play perfect strength down the table to leave the cue ball tidily tucked behind the yellow.

If the ball touching the cue ball is not a ball 'on' (e.g., if the striker is on a red and the cue ball is touching black), the touching-ball rule is irrelevant as the player still has to strike a ball 'on' and must not disturb the black in any event. Of course, in playing away from the black he doesn't hit it and is not deemed to have hit it. Referees are occasionally seen declaring 'Touching ball' in these situations, but strictly speaking they shouldn't say anything because the touching-ball rule doesn't apply. Most referees know this. Some of them will refuse to answer if the player asks if it's a touching ball. In so doing they are probably being over-correct. Although the question and answer are strictly immaterial, the player wants to know and what's the harm in telling him? His question is on 'a fact connected with play' and under the rules the referee shall decide any question of fact connected with play, if asked.

Nap

Billiard cloth is made of wool and on the surface of the table the texture of the cloth, or nap, has an effect upon the way the balls behave. This texture, which might be compared to very short grass if it were examined microscopically, must be brushed and ironed before play, but during play, as the players' bridge hands pull it about, marks and tracks can be seen on the table like skid marks on a road. These are apparent because the nap has been moved from its original position.

When the cloth is laid on the table it is always laid with the fibres smoothed down from the bottom of the table towards the top. When a player is cueing from the bottom of the table to the top, therefore, the cue ball is said to be going 'with the nap'. Playing down the table, against the direction in which the fibres are lying, is 'against the nap'.

In Europe, America and Canada the slight variations in play which the nap causes are disliked and on their tables they use nylon or similar materials which give a smooth 'bald' finish with very little or no nap. But the nap is a feature of a British billiard table and every player must learn to use it to his advantage and to understand the subtle and delightful differences it can make.

Normally the effect of nap is only seen in shots played at a gentle pace. In high-speed shots the nap has little effect. A full explanation of the effects of nap would require a separate chapter, but if you watch a top player playing a gentle stroke up or down the table (nap has little effect across the table) you may come to appreciate that the ball did not just luckily roll off its expected line – it was made to do so by the player cunningly making use of nap.

The loose red

A term used in most cases when the pack of reds is fairly tight and both players are trying to force an error from one another by clever placing of the cue ball in awkward positions. Eventually a mistake is made and a red will be loosened from the pack, drifting into an open position. This red can so often hold the key to the frame, giving the first man to get a chance of potting it the ascendancy in the frame.

Take note of the number of times you see a careless break of the pack at the opening of a frame when a red or two are chipped out unintentionally. The next player makes a good pot and proceeds to dominate the frame, thus possibly setting the pattern of play for a session. Quite often a situation can arise where one player is dominating play and full of confidence and his opponent, only too aware of the fact, is playing continual safety, returning the cue ball to the baulk end and trying to tuck up on the bottom cushion. In such a case the dominant player may allow a couple of loose reds to be pushed around the lower-scoring colours in the 'D' area to make his opponent's safety play more hazardous, thus applying more pressure.

These are just a few of the terms you may hear in use during a snooker commentary. It is the viewer's prerogative to say, 'I don't think he knows what he's talking about,' but perhaps this complaint will now be voiced less often.

4
The Karnehm Method

I was fortunate to be brought up in an atmosphere which encouraged the attainment of billiard skills from an early age. My father owned a fairly large house on the north side of London with a huge garden which he cultivated and nurtured into a delightful area; we had a billiard table on which he also cultivated quite a high skill. Add to these facts the existence of my four older brothers, all very capable players, and it is easy to see that I was never short of opposition not only from the tip end of the cue but very often from the butt end as well!

We were visited frequently by Tom Newman, in my eyes the most proficient billiard player of all time, and his brother Stanley, also a professional who never reached the heights of his brother. Tom, admired greatly by the incomparable Walter Lindrum, was a true gentleman of the billiard world; rather mild in manner and not a robust man, his pleasure was to stroll in the fields enjoying the simple life. Sadly, he died in his early forties. During his visits to us Tom would become immersed in the garden for a while, eventually returning to give me a lesson on the finer arts of billiards. The floor lino around the table had a join at the centre pocket, providing a perfect guide to the placement of the feet when potting into the opposite centre pocket. It is a memory which is very clear to me, possibly because of Tom's emphasis of correct stance in relation to this seam in the lino.

That was in 1924, but it was not until 1973 that the idea of using a tape across the table continuing along the floor to take the place of the lino seam occurred to me. In coaching manuals lines are sometimes drawn on photos and diagrams for guidance, but this is not quite the same thing as practical tuition, and the tape method is a simple but extremely effective measure in practice. Now of course the idea has been adopted by the National Coaching Scheme and Foundation and is part of every area coach's equipment.

In the past coaching was never really taken seriously as a means of improving your game more quickly. The usual method was to find a good player and copy him or try to obtain a few hints as best you could. If he had bad habits, that was your hard luck: what worked for him might not work for you. A really top player usually has neither the time nor the inclination to give information, if indeed he has the ability to impart his knowledge. Coaching is not a series of instructive sessions to make all players look alike; it is more a moulding of a person's abilities into a position that suits the build and a style most likely to bring success which conforms as near as possible with the accepted ideas of play. The purpose of a single proven method available to enthusiasts around the country is to eliminate, to a large extent, the dangers of the barrack-room-lawyer type who gives misguided notions, based on his own limited experience of play, to gullible youngsters. This can create habits which, once established, become extremely hard to break, limiting a potential of who knows what.

Once young players have been helped to develop their stance and style to a sound degree of correctness, it is mostly down to them to continue to seek greater accuracy in everything else they do. As their touch and ability improve, so will the shots appear that at one time they could not recognize. Their own inventiveness will set the pattern of their game, and their character and temperament will govern to some extent their ability to perform.

The one thing common to all players of high standard who find they have lost form is a return to the basics to iron out faults. Mental stress, whatever its cause, will often break down the co-ordination and timing mechanisms, causing a movement or snatch somewhere in the cueing action. It stands to reason, therefore, that the better your understanding of technique and of yourself, the more the likelihood of a return to form, with some slight adjustment to the works.

So where does it all start? First of all, we must establish the main points of the overall stance technique in the normal playing position at the table. Let me take you, with the help of photographs, through the tape, which is a continuation of the line of aim along which you must learn to propel the cue like a piston. The stance that you adopt in the correct position, with any slight adaptations you may make to suit your own body, will give you feelings and tensions that no one can teach you but yourself – so cultivate them, and you will create good playing habits.

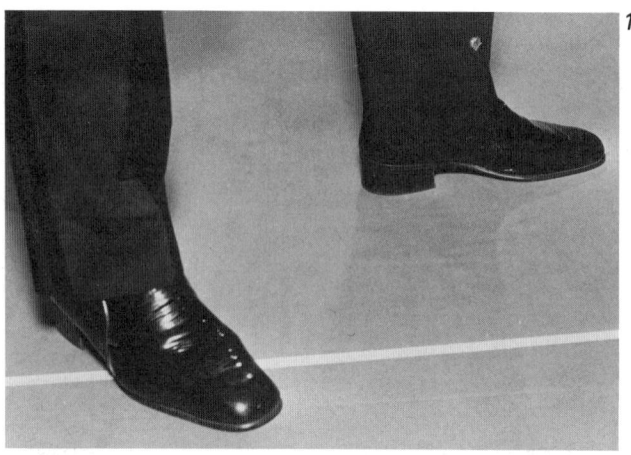

1 1 Correct stance. Right foot on line of aim, left foot parallel to line of aim. Note the distance you feel that slightly exerts you when you twist to get down to the shot. Firm and solid.
  2 Not quite good enough. Left foot not parallel.
  3 Left foot too close to line of aim. Common fault. Loss of balance.
  4 Both feet wrong. Too close together.
  5 Both feet wrong, left foot especially. Very bad balance all round.

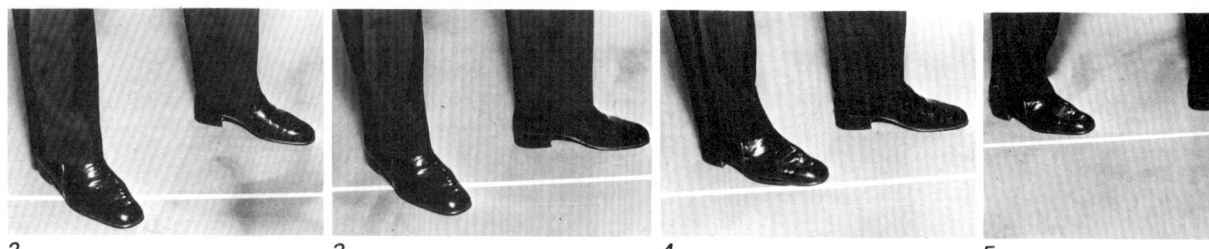

2   *3*   *4*   *5*

6

7

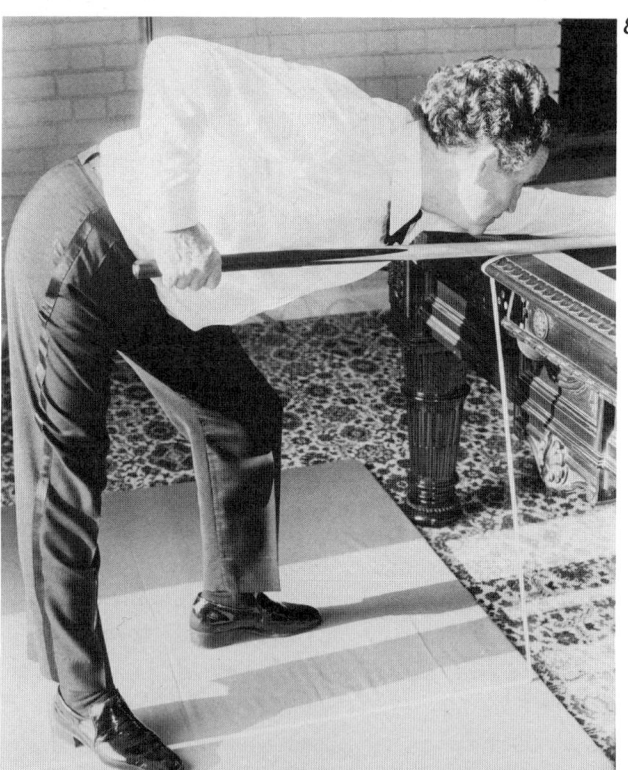

8 6 Correct. If the feet are positioned correctly, as in Plate 1 above, the body will be placed facing away from the line of shot.
  7 Body twist. Try not leaning away from the line before getting down.
  8 Complete stance.

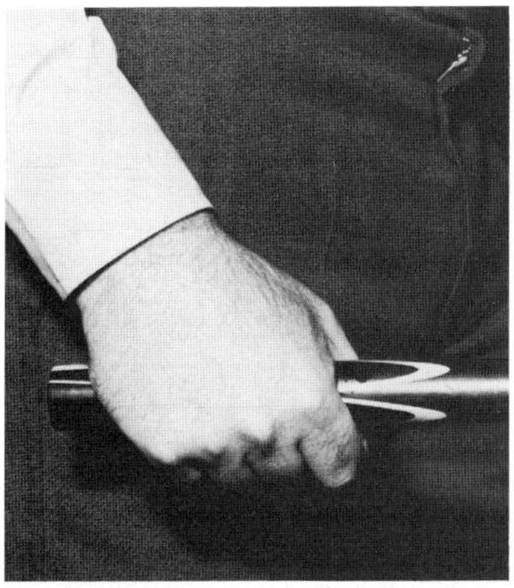

9 Normal cue butt hold. Soft but firm.
10 Bridge arm fully extended creates solid frame when combined with action described in 7 opposite.
11 Bridge arm gaining further support by resting forearm on the table. Note strong bridge hand.
12 Front-on view. Elbow line straight. Cue on line.

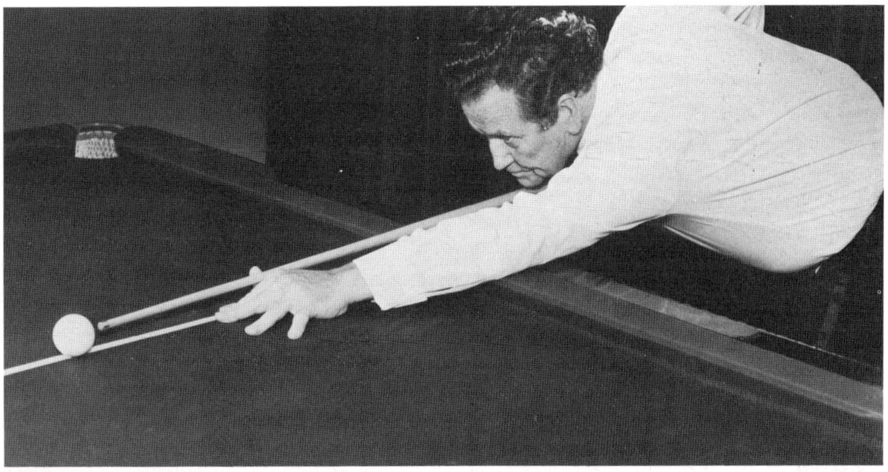

Effects of cue-ball striking

Before we get too involved in the effects of side and all its possibilities in stroke making, let us try to establish a mutual agreement on one or two of the principles involved. Much has been written over the years as to its action and possible reaction on either cue ball or object balls. Scientists have explored and expounded their theses, all of which are informative in terms of knowledge alone. Even top players have agreed not to agree on some aspects of the imparting of side from one ball to another. I do not intend to do anything but explain my practical experience of the effect of side as found when playing on the type of cloth used for the English game of billiards. The effects will apply equally to snooker played under the same conditions.

To apply side to the cue ball means to strike it off-centre to the left or right to ensure that it does not roll forward on a true vertical axis. On any given line of aim there can only be one centre of the cue ball, so it is fair to assume that a player striking

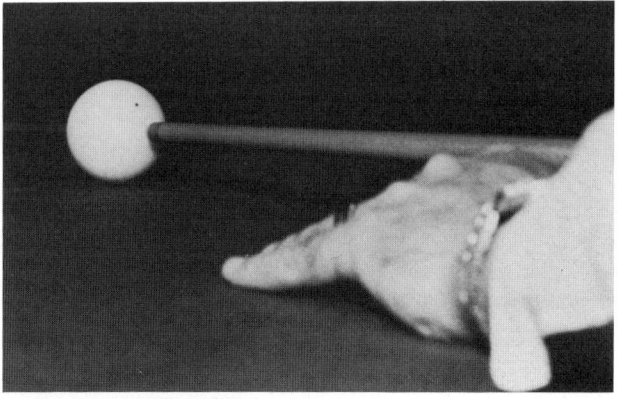

13 Centre ball striking.

anywhere other than dead centre, which is a very small area indeed, is imparting side to the cue ball whether intended or not. Therein lies the almost hidden secret of this teasing game, for if you do not strike the cue ball where you intended, either centre or off-centre, you are not on the correct line of aim with your cue at the precise moment of striking.

TOP SPIN

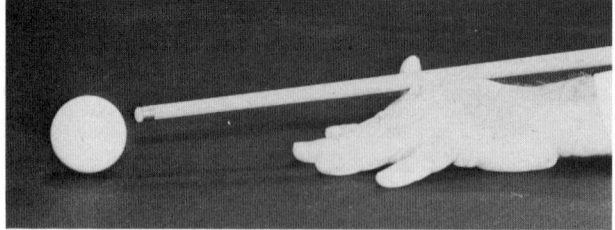

To strike above true centre, as indicated, will set the cue ball rolling in a forward motion. At the highest point of contact, the greatest amount of forward or top spin will be imparted to the ball. On the bed of the table it will give a gripping effect to the ball on the nap of the cloth, particularly if you are playing with the nap. Much depends on the skill of the player as to how much effect can be achieved by quality of cue action and accurate striking of the cue ball.

It must be realized that a ball loaded with top spin, upon striking a cushion straight on, will on reversing its direction of travel also reverse its effect, so that top becomes back spin until it is expended, allowing the ball to roll in a forward motion.

Once the feel of producing this heavy spin is effected, it is amazing the number of shots that can be added to your repertoire which at some time will come to your aid. You will discover that a powerful top-spin shot will maintain its spin after contact with another ball and still have strong effect off a cushion as long as the object ball and cushion are close together.

BACK-SPIN AND DRAG SHOTS

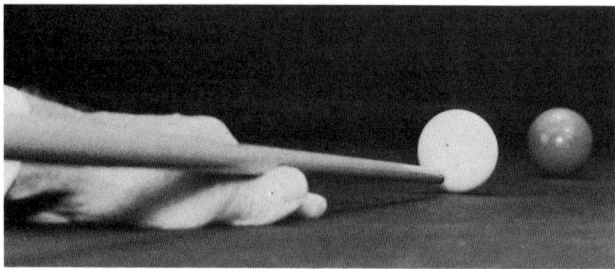

Low striking for screw effect.

Backspin is produced by striking the cue ball below centre on the vertical axis, either just low or very low. This will send the cue ball forward on the line of aim selected with reverse or back spin. According to how low you strike the ball and how well you perform the action, so the cue ball will respond to your demands. The action of the cue ball will depend on the power put into the shot. At the moment of striking, the ball skids forward approximately 12 or 18 inches, just sitting on its vertical axis – that is the initial power of the strike; it then proceeds further to the halfway stage, still with back spin which then peters out, allowing the forward rotation to take over, whence the cue ball runs freely to its intended target.

The purpose of this shot, which is referred to as a 'drag', is to maintain longer control of cue-ball action when playing a shot of full table length before contacting the object ball. The initial faster speed at which the shot is played is reduced by the back spin before natural rolling commences. Drag dispenses with the long, slow shot which can be chancy, especially on uneven tables with bad spots which can cause the ball to lose direction on its way. It is always dangerous to roll the cue ball on long shots at a pace that will not overcome nap effect. Remember that fingermarks caused by strong bridge hands thrust against the nap in a careless fashion ruck it up and create havoc with slow shots. This bad habit is common among snooker players in general; it is unnecessary and only spoils the playing surface for the more discerning player.

SIDE SPIN

Left-hand side.

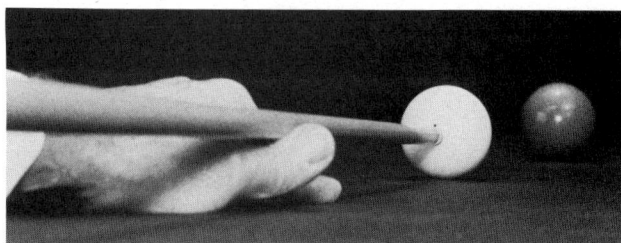

A hint of right-hand side.

Striking to the left of centre will send the cue ball on its forward journey spinning off its vertical axis in a clockwise direction. Striking below the centre line will increase the spin as the forward rotation axis leans further away from the true vertical axis in its clockwise spin. This can soon be grasped by a reasonably new player. Of course, the same rule also applies in reverse, using right-hand-side striking of the cue ball. Playing up and down the table will soon establish these facts. Remember that with these side shots it is the cue that does the work, not the muscle power of your arm. Propel the cue in a sliding motion – practice will improve this.

The point not appreciated by most players is that

when side is used, a 'push-away' from the selected line of aim takes place. Now, if the shot is played at the correct pace, which allows the nap of the cloth to pull the ball back on to line, the object-ball contact will be correct. A misjudgement of pace or bad cueing, however, will probably make the contact too thick or thin, thereby not giving the anticipated result. The required pace depends on the distance between the two balls involved. The long shot requires great judgment in assessing the amount of swing the cue ball takes when using side, and the power of the shot will vary the amount of swing that occurs. The nap, which is different on every table, will have a varying effect on the curve that takes place. This 'push-off' effect makes aiming a most complicated exercise. It is fair to say that many players possess natural judgment in these matters and improve quickly with guidance, yet many can spoil any rhythm of play and timing with which they might be endowed by concentrating too hard on the theory. So much depends on the individual needs of players regarding pleasure and how they seek it.

SCREW EFFECTS

The action of a screw shot is similar to the drag shot. If an object ball is placed 2 feet in front of the path of the cue ball and struck as for the drag shot, the screw back will be effected. The power of the screw or back spin imparted to the cue ball in all shots of this nature is dependent on good cue action and perfect timing of the delivery; the muscle power of the arm which has to be used to perform the shot must not be allowed to become part of the cue as it strikes the ball. If your cue hold or muscle reflexes are tight in the hand holding the butt at the precise moment of impact, the screw or spin effect will be lost to a large extent. At the moment of contact with the cue ball, the butt hand should be merely guiding the cue on its true line, allowing the cue only to cause its effects on the ball by its low contact and follow-through action. The butt hand employs the same wrist action required in throwing a hoop forward a few feet in such a way as to make it spin back to you, the backward spin taking effect at the end of its forward thrust.

At a close distance of 18 inches the screw effect can be practised in a gentle manner until the action is mastered. This exercise will teach you to master butt control precisely.

It is wise to remember that side screw, etc., can always be risky and should be used only when really necessary. I know all players find its use fascinating, and many rely on its effect too heavily in the belief that good players use it all the time. This is quite mistaken and is the cause of most prospective players' downfall. The further the object ball is away from the cue ball, the more difficult it is to achieve screw effects. The skill to drive the cue ball forward, say 6 feet, maintaining enough power and back spin on it until it strikes the object ball, is not usually found in the general club player. Nor is it of any use to be able to get the action unless accuracy is also obtained. You can soon find the limits of accuracy to which you are able to play, and set your standard.

Place your cue ball on the baulk line and the object ball 12 inches in front for a straight pot into the top corner pocket. Pot the object ball and screw back into the corner pocket under your butt. Gradually increase the distance of the shot until you have the object ball on the blue spot, keeping the cue ball on the baulk line for all the shots, still trying to pocket the object ball and the cue ball as in the first instance. You will soon realize the need for sound technique in your stance and delivery.

The power or force of a screw shot may be described as 'soft' or 'deep'. A soft screw shot, as the word implies, is a delicate or gentle stroke, but it must always be played with conviction. Deep screw, on the other hand, requires force, a word I do not like using: to the average player, force means muscle, which immediately involves all the culprits of bad cueing, such as gripping the butt too tightly or snatching, creating the jerky action which every player tries to overcome.

Much depends on the distance between cue and object ball with screw shots. A deep screw played when the balls are only 12 inches or so apart can be achieved with tremendous power and effect by many players, simply because in the first instant the correct contact on the object ball with the cue ball is more easily achieved over a short distance and, just as important, the power or spin applied to the cue ball is not lost or exhausted over the short distance it has to travel. If the balls are 4 feet or more apart, the application of power and back spin combined with accuracy is very demanding of sound technique and also first-rate timing.

I took part in an experiment which aimed to explain the action of balls on certain materials, and much to everyone's surprise I was able to obtain strong screw back effects on a glass surface, yet on a carborundum surface with balls also impregnated with carborundum powder the effect was almost nil and friction seemed to be eliminated almost as if the balls were engaged in a wheel cog. In an extremely slow-action film (the cue ball travelled 18 inches in about twenty-five seconds) I played a deep screw to observe cue-ball action. The shot played was as follows: the cue ball, 18 inches behind the blue on its spot, was screwed back to the end cushion with maximum power. On contact, the cue ball stopped dead, turning four complete revolutions on the spot before gripping the nap and spinning backwards, and as the distance between the cue ball and object ball was increased the back spin was partly lost and the screw effect diminished. The same shot played on glass had a similar effect as on cloth, but obtaining correct contact on the object ball proved difficult due to skidding of the cue ball on its way to the object ball.

CHECK OR RUNNING SIDE

Check or running side are expressions commonly used in conversation or commentary to describe the use or effect of side applied to the cue ball when playing a shot. In general terms its purpose is to apply spin to the cue ball in such a way that when the cue ball strikes its first cushion it will either extend the angle of throw off that cushion, or restrict or narrow the angle off the cushion. The aim is to effect a positioning of the cue ball for the shot to follow, when this might be difficult or impossible to achieve by plain ball striking.

Now, before you reach for pen and paper, let me say that that is a simple explanation of side effect. It would suffice to say that check side restricts the angle of the cue ball in the direction it is travelling, and running side extends the angle, and leave it at that. However, the great mystery in the world of snooker, at least to the majority of players, is how to cope with the use of side and all the strange effects it can have, completely altering the intended effects of a shot. Not only does it alter the path of the cue ball, it affects the path of the object ball as well. Add to that the effect of nap, which varies from table to table, and there is little wonder we all have problems.

Perhaps it is well to appreciate that probably the most difficult thing to do is strike the cue ball in its perfect centre. Why? Because there is only one centre. Therefore every shot which has not been struck perfectly – and such shots are in the majority – has a degree of misdirection involved in its execution. This is less of a problem to professionals because of their higher standard of striking than the average player who is far less accurate and as a consequence has many more unaccountable misses. Side, its use and effects, could stand a volume on its own to satisfy the enthusiast.

Bridge hands

What is the first thing you look for when playing a new opponent? Personally, I look for the bridge

BRIDGE HANDS

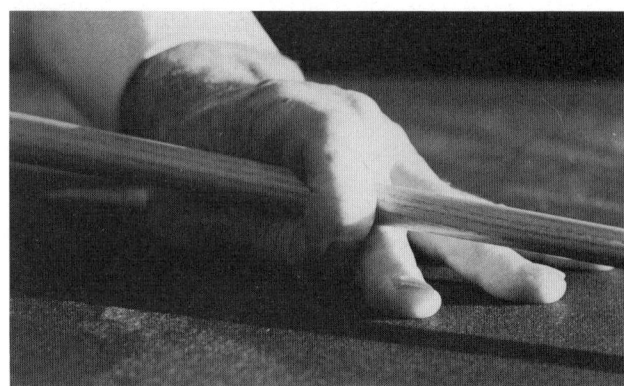

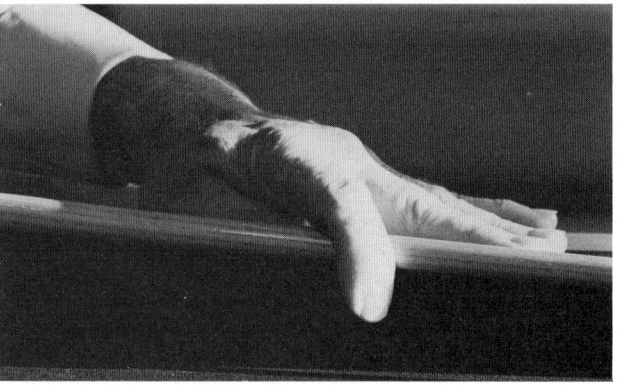

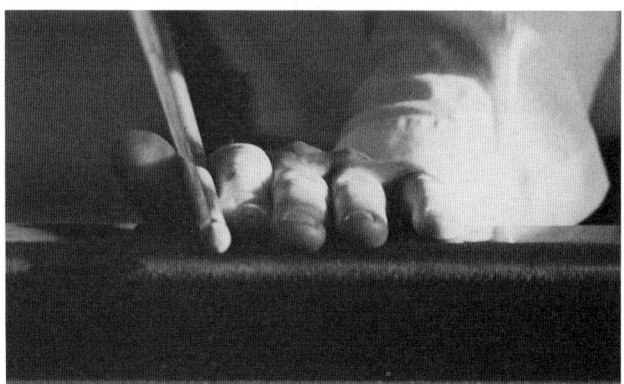

Note the deep groove made to prevent the cue escaping the hand in what is always a difficult situation.

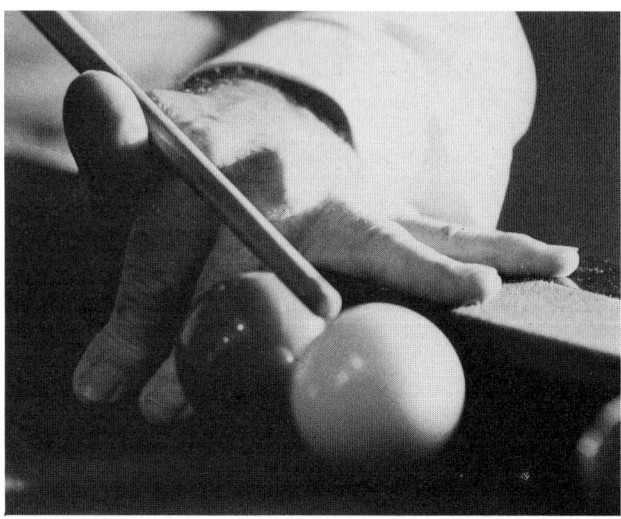

Another awkward situation, in which inventiveness can be a virtue. Remember to keep the hand firm.

THE KARNEHM METHOD

How to bridge over an awkward set of balls.

hand which to me conveys a great deal about the ability and type of player opposing me.

First, the bridge hand should be firm and strong: it can express the confidence felt by the player performing. If it is weak-looking and sloppy, his game will be played on similar lines. Everyone appreciates the value of a soft but positive hold of the butt, so here is a tip for you next time you play. Put as much pressure as you can on the finger pads of your bridge hand and you will feel a natural ease come into your butt hand which allows the wrist to function a little more sweetly. Reverse the procedure and you will find a soft bridge hand cultivates a tighter butt hand.

As in all aspects of play, personal likes and dislikes, with whatever natural aptitudes you have, will play their part in allowing you to improvise with your bridge hand. Forming a sound bearing through which your cue can run freely is something which will develop whatever position you find your hand needs to take.

The basic bridge hand as shown in the photographs, with variations off the cushions, can be utilized in many ways. It is important always to be firm and strong in the hand. It is also worth saying that a cardinal sin committed by most snooker players, including some professionals, is to drag the hand back off the table after the shot. This careless action, especially when done against the nap, can have an adverse effect on many of the more delicate shots that have to be played when great accuracy is demanded, so just *lift* your hand off the table. Many a good cue action has been blamed for missing a shot when in fact the delivery has been spoilt not by action, but by a movement or twitch of the bridge hand steering the cue so slightly off its original line.

The Americans, when playing their game of pool, use the looped finger bridge. Pool demands slightly more punch in the delivery, which can cause an exaggeration of any movement that might take place. I have heard expert American pool players say it has been a natural development in eliminating cue movement. They do, of course, play with thicker and heavier cues and larger balls; nevertheless I have often wondered why our players have not used their method more, particularly with long deep screw shots and the like. The cue can certainly be prevented from escaping the normal 'V' of the thumb and forefinger. The photographs illustrate a type of looped bridge, with the cue running along the thumb and pad of the middle finger and the forefinger pressing on to those bearings.

Shots for your locker

Shot A

This shot occurs, often causing an easy miss, from what appears to be a comparatively simple pot (if there is such a thing). The problem really is not potting the ball, but getting the cue ball out of the corner due to the straightness of the line of aim. By taking the cushion first you will find that the pot is not as difficult as you thought, and this method also gives you more scope to move the cue ball around.

Never be too ambitious when the object ball is further from the pocket than indicated: a little practice will teach a lot. Beware also of when the object ball is well into the jaw of the pocket, as a complete miss is deceptively easy to achieve; so aim up to the ball. This is a shot more likely to be overlooked than actually missed.

Shot B

A plant-type shot, potting the ball nearest to the

centre pocket, even the chap on the window sill in the photograph could knock this one in! Strike the top ball a crisp contact on its right side and the lower ball will gently proceed to its destination, the centre pocket, without fail. These shots are unobserved far too often by club players, due to lack of knowledge rather than lack of ability.

Shot C

This is another example of a plant – not as obvious as the normal straight-line plant, but just as simple to execute. By playing at the outside edge of the centre ball on its right side, a gentle shot will send it into the corner pocket. Soft screw will not impair the result in any way, but merely gives you greater scope with positioning of the cue ball.

Shot D

This shot demonstrates the Massé stroke, seldom used in snooker, the object being to create a swerve around the object ball of 180° to strike another ball, or both balls if a cannon is being played in billiards. It is not a shot I would advise you to play in the club as mistakes can rather bruise the cloth. Generally players strike this shot much too hard. The effect is to apply deep screw from the vertical position, skidding the cue ball out from the object ball with enough side effect to pull it back around the object ball in a semi-circle. The elbow should be tucked

All photos in this chapter by John Carty.

into the side for firmness, with the hand turned, creating a strong firm tripod of fingers to keep the cue on line and steady. The pressure of the cue against the thumb is such that if it were suddenly taken away the cue would spring forward into the table. The Massé, of course, is exploited to the full in 'artistic billiards', as played best by the Belgians who are able to develop tremendous spin power. They play a series of shots which carry points according to the difficulty ratio and the winner is the player with most marks, a system similar to that used in diving competitions in the swimming world.

Walter Lindrum played Massé shots extremely consistently, mainly because of his close cannon ability. If he got a cover he would raise his butt and go through the motion as if it were a normal shot. The shot I most admired, however, which I have managed myself, was played with comparative ease by Clarke Macconachy, the former New Zealand professional champion. He could Massé completely round the triangle, sending the cue ball from a starting position on one side of the base up that side, around the apex and down the other side. Unless you want a hole in your cloth, I would advise you not to try it!

5

Meet the new professionals

It is the ambition of many good snooker players to become professionals. Nowadays there are lads of twelve and thirteen years old who have a professional career firmly in mind, and the best of them will not be disappointed in their aims. During the last few years many of the best amateurs have experienced a rejection of their application to turn professional, but in 1981 the floodgates opened and many more players were accepted into the professional ranks than in any other year in the history of the game.

To become a recognized professional player it is necessary to become a member of the World Professional Billiards and Snooker Association (WPBSA),* the governing body of professional snooker. This association's committee is made up of the world's top pros and they consider every application. In the last five or six years their decisions on whom to accept or reject have been erratic and difficult to justify, but more recently they have made a determined effort to achieve some sort of consistency in their approach.

Their problem is that they cannot admit players of mediocre ability as that would be bad for the game; on the other hand they cannot (or at least should not) reject players just because they have not won every amateur title available. A rigid approach, for example in insisting that applicants must have won the World or English Amateur Championship (and this was tried), is too restrictive and leads to the obvious criticism that not all of the professional players who sit in judgment won these titles – or anything comparable – when they were amateurs. At the end of 1980 it was decided that the current batch of applicants for the professional ranks should compete in a qualifying tournament, the winner to be accepted as a professional. This was still restrictive because it meant that the only new professionals in a year would be the winner of this tournament, the winner of the world title (only held every two years) and the winner of the English championship, a possible total of three new faces per year.

The first qualifying tournament was held at Sheffield Snooker Centre and was won by Dave Martin of Peterlee, County Durham. Dave

*WPBSA Ltd since November 1981.

therefore had good cause to be pleased with this arrangement and in fact he went on to become the most successful new professional of the year, apart from Jimmy White who had turned professional late in 1980, but others were less pleased. Jack Fitzmaurice of Birmingham, a former England international with a long and distinguished amateur record, refused to take part in the tournament. He had applied for professional status on numerous occasions and been rejected. He felt that his record alone was enough and that it was demeaning to the top amateurs to oblige them to play in a tournament that could only produce a winner, not decide who was actually well fitted to be a professional player.

Within weeks of the end of this controversial tournament the WPBSA had a change of heart and accepted five applications. A month later they accepted a further batch of thirteen players, including six Scots who had been prepared to set up their own professional association. The new approach was that, in addition to the big amateur title winners who had previously been acceptable, the WPBSA would accept players who had played for their country or had won a 'prestigious tournament'. This allowed most people with professional ambitions to turn professional immediately, although others were still rejected.

However, the Home International Championship includes the Isle of Man as a separate team. As it has a population smaller than most English counties, the island produces a 'national' team of about English county standard. If the new rule were applied literally, the entire Isle of Man team could turn professional, the thought of which, despite the sportsmanship and enthusiasm of the Isle of Man players, would be enough to give most professionals nightmares. So the 'international' test is rather more stringent than it appears. It is difficult to discern an exact criterion; Tommy Murphy, Northern Ireland Champion, was accepted, but Paul Watchorn of Dublin, who had played for his country five times, was rejected; 1981 Republic of Ireland Champion Tony Kearney was also rejected.

The basis of selection can still be criticized but the WPBSA have accepted most of the deserving applicants and under their new policies will surely accept those amateur players with a strong record in their own country. The game needs new faces and, apart from the additional problems caused by having large numbers of competitors in every tournament – which is purely an administrative problem of no significance to anyone but the promoter – it is all to the good of the game, even if we eventually have a hundred or a hundred and fifty professional players. They can't all become champions, they can't all make a full-time living from snooker, but they can at least be given the chance of fulfilling their ambitions because they are all good players and one of 'the class of 1981' could well be a World Champion of the future.

One of the effects of the increased number of professional players (others will show up throughout the game) is that it is almost impossible to keep track of them all individually. In this chapter we introduce just some of the new professionals and in doing so we do not imply that these are the best or the most interesting of the new crop. To do full justice to them all would take up half of this book, and much as we respect and admire them all we're not ready for that just yet!

Dave Martin

Photo: John Carty.

Dave Martin of Peterlee, County Durham, has made a determined effort to gain his own place in the professional ranks, and in his first year he qualified for the Embassy World Championship, losing to Bill Werbeniuk when he 'froze' under the glare of the television lights. He had a string of impressive wins to earn £5,000 as losing semi-finalist (to Dennis Taylor) in the Jameson Open in September 1981. He has now moved from County Durham to take over as manager and resident professional at Mike Watterson's Sheffield Snooker Centre. This is a new trend in the game whereby professionals, as in golf, can be attached to a club, make a good living and, if they're lucky, have plenty of opportunity for practice. There are now about twenty players with such a club arrangement – something that was virtually unknown a few years ago.

Dave's career is anything but typical. He started playing snooker as a boy and reached a good standard, but he then joined the Merchant Navy which naturally took him well away from snooker. In all he spent nearly six years at sea, an experience he enjoyed, but was drawn back to the game when he settled in High Wycombe, Bucks, in 1974. One evening he went into the local club and watched a game between two players he didn't know but who turned out to be Mike Darrington and Patsy Fagan. Dave started playing again and, in practice against these top amateurs, especially Darrington, he soon raised his game to a high level. When the Ron Gross Centre opened in North London in 1975 Dave was a regular player there and had the chance to practise against the best players in London.

He returned to the North-East and built up a reputation in regional tournaments, in the leagues and in the Durham county team. By 1979 he had a very solid record of tournament success and in the English Amateur Championship he went all the way to the final, meeting Jimmy White of London in Helston, Cornwall. It was an epic match but in the end the young Londoner won the title. Dave was back the following year, again reaching the final of the toughest tournament in the amateur game. He met Joe O'Boye of Leicester in the final at Milton Keynes, Bucks, and as the better-known and more experienced player was a favourite to beat the twenty-year-old Midlander. But he did not play with any real conviction and Joe O'Boye beat him to become English Champion.

Dave then set his sights on the professional game and won the professional qualifying tournament at Sheffield, beating Tony Graham of Grimsby, Ian Williamson of Leeds and, in the final, Eugene Hughes of Dublin. He has come a long way since his days at sea and has made the difficult transition to the professional game in fine style. When all the controversy about the admittance or rejection of new men was in the air, another newcomer, Geoff Foulds of London, said, 'I'll wager anyone that of this and the last batch of professionals, at least three will make it to the very highest ranks. I don't know which three, but in a few years time we'll all know.' Dave Martin is already well on the way to claiming one of those few places.

MEET THE NEW PROFESSIONALS

Vic Harris

Photo: John Carty.

Vic Harris had been one of the leading amateurs in the South of England since 1973. Six times Essex champion, a stalwart of the Essex County team and a successful campaigner in money matches, he had been unlucky in the English Championship, usually qualifying for the later stages but losing within sight of the final. In 1981 he at last won the title that always seemed likely to elude him, the English Amateur Championship, when he beat George Wood of County Durham 13-9 at Milton Keynes, Bucks. Vic, the most likeable and modest of men, had played a large part in 'bringing on' the young Steve Davis, acting as his sparring partner in thousands of frames of snooker at the Lucania Club, Romford. While this experience benefited Vic – as it did Steve – it left him with the unshakeable opinion that he would never be as good as Steve Davis and to some extent this undermined his confidence in his own game. But he was, without doubt, one of England's top players. At least since 1976 it has been possible to claim that he is one of the five best long potters in the world, amateur or professional, and in money matches against Alex Higgins (receiving the amateur's customary 14 points start) Vic has a better record than anyone against the Hurricane.

Vic started playing snooker as a lad at Romford Lucania but, in a pattern typical of many players, he gave up the game from the age of eighteen until he was twenty-five in favour of courtship and marriage. He began to play again at the Lucania Club in Barkingside, but soon moved back to Romford where Barry Hearn, chairman of the Lucania chain of snooker clubs, was starting to take an interest in competitive snooker. Vic was the darling of Romford, and in a series of challenge matches he showed his winning power and popularity as the local boys turned out in force to see him play.

He is a thoughtful and provocative talker on all aspects of the game but has never been known to say a bad word about anyone. He is a real East-Ender and his accent makes it necessary for non-Londoners to listen to him with some care. Part of his sense of humour is to make up his own words and phrases as he goes along and he will deliberately exaggerate his accent if it will get a laugh. On a visit to Canada in 1980 he insisted on talking to his taxi driver in the broadest tones he could manage. The driver had expressed some interest in snooker but couldn't understand a word Vic said and he looked to Vic's fellow passengers to act as interpreters. Unfortunately he 'looked' too literally and often and the passengers, equally convulsed with laughter and stricken by terror, had physically to push the driver's head round to get his eyes back on the road. But the driver was mesmerized, 'What's he talking – Polish? Czech? Come on, what?' The passengers assured him that Vic was speaking English. 'Ain't nobody can talk like that and be speaking English,' the driver said, shaking his head in wonder.

The six-foot-seven-inches-tall Vic is English to the tips of his toes, and his amateur career was capped by his being selected to play in the England team in 1979 and 1980. He is managed by Barry Hearn of Lucania, who also manages Steve Davis and Tony Meo, and with that support and his own immense talents he will make his presence felt in the professional game – even if, with his usual modesty, he makes it sound as if he's just come along to watch the 'real' professionals.

Colin Roscoe

Colin Roscoe of Connah's Quay in Flint, had been at or near the top of amateur snooker since 1974, but being based in North Wales he was unable to benefit fully from all the increased action in South Wales because of the distance involved. While snooker in the valleys was booming and many Welsh players were improving by great strides, Colin was virtually the only top-class player in

North Wales and had to look to Liverpool for his match experience.

Colin was North Wales Champion, Deeside Champion and Liverpool Invitation Champion in 1981. He was selected to play for Wales in 1980 and turned professional in 1981. He is an attractive attacking player with a highest break of 146, and despite the great strength of South Wales, Colin ended his amateur days by becoming the first player from North Wales to win the coveted Welsh title, beating Elwyn Richards of Barry in the final.

In his new professional career he is assisted by the well-known referee John Williams, who acts as his manager.

Dean Reynolds

Dean Reynolds of Grimsby has come through to the professional ranks with a speed that is breathtaking. He is only nineteen years old and was steadily building up a reputation on the amateur circuit. He was chosen to play for England in the Home Internationals Series at Pontins in 1981. However, in April of that year Dean had won the television 'Junior Pot Black' tournament – a one-frame match with many of the world's best youngsters taking part – and such is the power of television that this one event changed the expected shape of his career.

In May he had won the British Under-19s Championship, beating Tommy Murphy of Northern Ireland in the final, and in June he scored a good win in a big senior tournament, the Stockton Buffs Pro-Am on Teeside, beating Malcolm Bradley of Stoke in the final. He had made his first maximum break at the age of seventeen, and with the departure of his neighbours Ray Edmonds, Sid Hood and Mike Hallett for the professional ranks he was in a position to dominate the very strong Grimsby area. It was a record that needed another year of senior competition and a good run in the England team, but Dean surprised the amateur world by applying to turn professional in September 1981 and the WPBSA surprised everyone by accepting him.

There is no doubt that Dean is a player of ability and potential, but he had not satisfied any of the criteria laid down by the WPBSA unless the one-frame 'lottery' of 'Junior Pot Black' is to be taken as a 'prestigious tournament'. There was one difference about Dean, however, he was and is very capably and sensibly handled by two friends from Grimsby, John Hare and Steve Bloomfield. They are snooker fanatics and although they are not professional managers in the class of the Mark McCormack Organization, they have promoted Dean in much the same way. No amateur player in England in 1981 enjoyed the backing and publicity

Photo: Humberside Promotions.

that Hare and Bloomfield put behind young Dean. Nothing was too much trouble, no booking too small to be overlooked, no challenge left unaccepted. They kept Dean busy with tours and exhibitions and made sure that he had every ounce of publicity they could obtain. It was a first-class exercise and, while it should have had no direct bearing on his professional application, it did something to lift him out of the ordinary run of good amateur players.

The WPBSA had decreed that it would consider new applicants only twice a year, in May and September, and Dean's managers assumed that if they applied in time for the September meeting his acceptance could be post-dated until he had completed his amateur commitments. This had been done in many recent cases, but it was unsatisfactory for players who had been officially accepted as professionals to play for a further month or two as amateurs, so the WPBSA also ended this practice – if they accepted Dean it would be with immediate effect. In some embarrassment his managers agreed to this, and Dean never did play for England.

In the enterprising hands of his managers Dean may well make a good living in the professional game. But it is a very different game from junior amateur tournaments and young Dean, like his townsman Mike Hallett before him, will have to do his 'apprenticeship' in the professional ranks. That worked for Hallett who is now, after more than two years as a professional, showing his true ability in major events. It should also work for 'Dashing Dean the potting machine' as he does have obvious potential But he will also need patience, and at nineteen that's a lot to ask.

Geoff Foulds

While London was producing the young superstars like Patsy Fagan, Steve Davis, Tony Meo and Jimmy White, the amateur game in the capital was dominated by Geoff Foulds of Perivale throughout the 1970s. He had a successful career in pools promotion and no ambitions to turn professional, so he was the mainstay of London snooker as the bright young men came up and went through to become professionals. He won the London Championship in 1971 and in every year from 1975 to 1979; he played for England with a good record from 1976 to 1979; and he was the captain of the London team that won the English county title on three occasions – and at one time or another he had each of the bright young men in his team. Although they outshone him eventually in the amateur game, he had good individual wins against all of them at

Photo: John Carty.

some stage in their careers. In the many one-day and two-day events held in London and Romford Geoff emerged as winner more often than not, and generally his record as an amateur in the South of England was an enviable one which has not been matched, over the same period, by any other player.

With the rise of the younger players, however, it seemed that Geoff's interest in the game was waning and it was a surprise to the snooker community when he turned professional. He admitted that he had 'gone stale' in the amateur game and sought admission to the paid ranks as a means of spurring himself on to greater endeavours. 'At every level of my career I have reached a stage when I started to go stale. Whether it was in league snooker, the county team or in individual tournaments, I reached a stage where I felt I could progress no further.'

Foulds had a bad start to his professional career, losing 5-2 in the Jameson Open qualifying round to another new pro, Doug French of Bolton. In his next outing, the Coral UK Championship, he scored his first professional success, beating yet another newcomer, Billy Kelly of Manchester, 9-7 and reaching the final of the qualifying group. In that match he lost 9-1 to the talented Tony Knowles of Bolton. 'I learned a lot from it,' Geoff said. 'Tony is a fine player and he was well on form, but when you start to play these 17-frame matches you realize just how different it is from the amateur game. A good amateur-style game is no longer enough. Young Tony was always good as an amateur, but he's made a quick transition to the pro ranks because even as an amateur he played in a professional style, going all out to score points and not getting bogged down in safety. In the long matches concentration plays a big part and that's something I'll have to work on. I went into it to learn and I think I've learned a lot already.'

Geoff is a founder member and permanent feature of the Ron Gross Centre in North London and he has played a part in developing London's young players. His seventeen-year-old son Neal has developed to become one of the top five or six players in London in 1981 and today Geoff and Neal must be the strongest father-and-son pairing in the world.

Geoff has never been one to rush into anything, on the table or off it, and he will take his time to weigh up the professional scene and his place within it. He may take more than the average two years to acclimatize fully to the harsher world of pro snooker, but once he's done that there is every chance that he will do as he did as an amateur – very nicely, thank you!

Eugene Hughes

Photo: John Carty.

Eugene Hughes of Dublin has been the Republic of Ireland's best prospect for quite some time. He was Irish Champion three times, has been a permanent feature of the Irish international team since 1975, and had a good record in his frequent competitive trips to England. He represented Ireland in the World Amateur Snooker Championship in Malta in 1978 and in Tasmania in 1980.

Like many Irishmen before him, Eugene came to London to seek his fortune (in 1977) and joined the group of outstanding young players then gathered at the Pot Black Club, Clapham, South London. He was too homesick to complete a full season in England, but before he went back to Dublin he improved his game in top-class competition and the experts agreed that here was a young man of style and potential.

The professional scene in Ireland is busier than it has ever been and Eugene has opportunities for exhibition and tournament play without having to move to England. In the last year alone, five new snooker clubs have opened in and around Dublin and some of the owners have plans for tournament action – which will do Eugene no harm.

He did fairly well in the Jameson Open, coming through from the depths of the qualifying group to the competition proper, but lost to the former World Amateur Champion, Ray Edmonds, 5-4 in a very close match. Eugene is managed by Pascal Burke, one of Ireland's top amateurs for over twenty years. One of the effects of the increased Irish activity is that a full-scale Irish Professional Championship can now be played, with seven other players trying to relieve Dennis Taylor of his title. In this championship Eugene will be joined by the other new professionals, Des Sheehan of Dublin, the Manchester-based Bill Kelly and Northern Ireland's Tommy Murphy. The old stagers making up the field of eight are Dennis Taylor, Alex Higgins, Patsy Fagan and Jack Rea. Ireland has never had as many as eight professionals before, but the interest, support and money are there now and it will be no surprise if Eugene, one of the few professionals actually living in Ireland, takes full advantage of them.

Dennis Hughes

Dennis Hughes of Manchester was a late starter in snooker: he first took up the game at the age of twenty, but soon developed into one of the leading players in the North of England. Throughout the 1970s his great rivals on the Lancashire scene were John Virgo and Paul Medati, and the three of them, together with George Scott of Liverpool, formed the Lancashire County team that won the English title in 1976. That year was a particularly good one for Dennis as he also won the Embassy Open Tournament, a national event that had no less than twelve thousand competitors taking part. His first prize in this was £500, the biggest of his career. 'We were hoping to make it a treble,' Dennis said. 'It was run in conjunction with the Embassy World Championship and at that time Alex Higgins, John Virgo and I played at Potters Club in Manchester. I won the Open, John won the big invitation tournament and Alex got to the final of the World Championship but lost to Ray Reardon.' In addition to this big win, Dennis has won the Manchester Championship five times and the Lancashire Championship twice, 'and that's more than John Virgo or Paul Medati did,' Dennis is

MEET THE NEW PROFESSIONALS

Photo: John Carty.

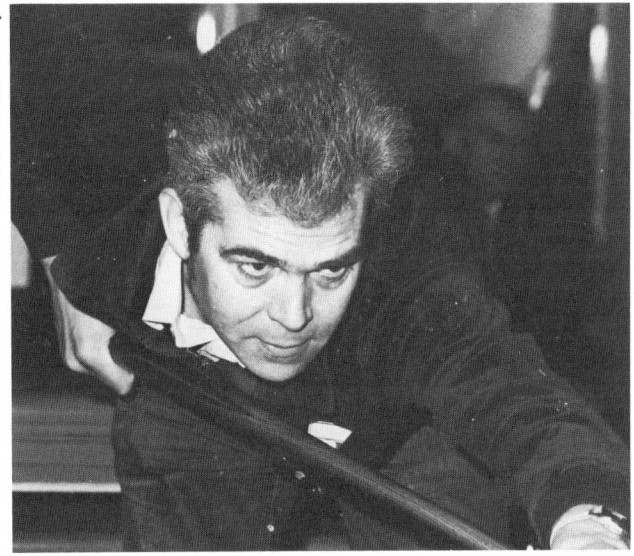

quick to point out. He won the Lancashire Pairs title once partnering John Virgo and twice partnering Bill Kelly, and in the latter half of the 1970s won every northern tournament of any note at one time or another. His highest break is 138, which he has achieved twice, and he has made nearly three hundred century breaks.

He too is part of the current trend, being resident player and manager at the Golden Leisure Snooker Centre in Manchester: 'It's a great thing for a professional like me. It gives me security and the chance to practise and maintain my game. It's good for the club owners because a name player pulls more members in and brings in good players. All the best clubs want their own resident professional nowadays and I think it's a great idea for all of us.'

Dennis's debut as a professional was in the Jameson Open where he beat experienced Jackie Rea but lost to another new professional, Bert Demarco of Edinburgh. In the Coral UK Championship he beat Vic Harris but lost in the next round to Mike Hallett.

Dennis is not worried about the supposed higher standard of the professional game: 'Most of the new professionals are the same people I've been playing for years as an amateur. I've played a lot of the top pros and I've nothing to fear from them if I'm playing well. The real difference I notice is that for a player like me there is much less activity in the professional game than there was in the amateur ranks: two or three major championships and some pro-ams if you can find them – it's not like competing nearly every week as an amateur.'

Manchester has always been one of the strongest centres of snooker in Britain and the new crop of professionals like Dennis will be aiming to keep it that way.

Joe Johnson

The success story of Joe Johnson of Bradford is one which new professionals might like to contemplate. Joe turned professional about fifteen months before the other players in this chapter, and in October 1981 he won the Youngers British Open Championship at Leeds – and this despite all sorts of personal problems, including a fire at his home. In the final he beat Cliff Wilson of Wales who had defeated him at their previous meeting – the final of the World Amateur Snooker Championship in Malta in 1979 – but this time Joe prevailed and earned his biggest-ever prize as a professional, £2,000.

Photo: John Carty.

6

Rules is rules

There are thought to be about fifty thousand clubs in the UK in which snooker and (to a lesser extent) billiards are played. In many of these clubs a game of snooker is a very friendly affair, an extension of a chat and a pint. The average standard of the players would make Ray Reardon weep, and in the 'knockabout' game, if the skills are not much in evidence, the rules are positively subverted. It is not a friendly action to tell your opponent that he has moved the green with his elbow when playing at a red, so nothing is said – the green was out of the way, didn't affect the shot and it's only a game, isn't it? If, however, the opponent is bold enough to claim a foul for this sort of shot in this sort of game, he's considered to be a spoilsport and things can become unfriendly. A serious dispute about the claimed foul is likely to be heated, idiotic and pointless, because neither player knows what he's talking about, has never read the rules and is unaware that in the darkest corner of the club hangs a sheet of rules which was placed there in 1937. So these friendly players develop rules of their own: 'The game hasn't started until the pack of reds has been hit'; 'It's not a foul to move another ball by less than 4 inches'; 'If you mis-hit the cue ball, you can have another go if it doesn't touch anything'.

In recent years things have improved, partly because of the influence of television, but mainly because most clubs have at least one competent player who plays in a league or in competitions and therefore knows something about the real rules of the games. Before the vast increase in the numbers of such players in recent times, the dispute would be solved by anyone who could express an opinion with sufficient force or volume. All serious players of any standard must know the rules. They are their protection and their guide. Many frames have been lost or won by ignorance or knowledge of the rules.

All competent players have a working knowledge of the rules and most of the professionals are as expert as any referee. But for all this modern enlightenment it must be said that with an estimated one million people playing the game in the UK alone, a vast proportion of games are still played under the rules according to Mickey Mouse and the only penalty for a ball elbowed 6 feet away is, 'Sorry, mate'.

The official rules of the games are owned and published by the Billiards & Snooker Control Council in booklet form, as broadsheets and in the informative but rather old-fashioned *B&SCC Handbook* (all obtainable from the B&SCC, 32 John William Street, Huddersfield, Yorks. Prices on application). The *Handbook* is overdue for revision but a new edition is unlikely to appear until late in 1982. Although the professional players are not affiliated to the B&SCC, they observe the published rules and any major alterations in the rules are discussed by both bodies. Unusually, in 1979 the professionals and amateurs failed to agree on a rule change. The B&SCC decided that in order to restrict the dominance of potting ability in billiards they would amend the rule which permitted the

Stan Brooke of Leeds, who was elected chairman of the B&SCC in 1981, following the death of Bill Cottier.

Photo: John Carty.

player to pot five reds off the spot to three reds only. This amendment came into force on 1 January 1979 but the professionals refused to go along with it and have their own 'two pots' rule in professional billiards, which may cause problems in official pro-am billiards events.

As the rules must be comprehensive – and as snooker is a comparative youngster – the rules are divided into three parts, the General Rules, the Rules of Billiards and the Rules of Snooker, and all have equal force. They are augmented and kept up to date by 'Official Decisions' which are discussed and proposed by the Rules Committee, passed by the full Council and published with the force of rules. The Official Decisions tend to govern set situations where the rule, although not requiring amendment, requires clarification in a particular case. For example, the rules say how the balls should be correctly spotted but an Official Decision provides that 'it is the striker's responsibility to see that [they] are correctly spotted before playing his stroke.'

There are many rules. They have been compiled over the years in a piecemeal way and there are inconsistencies within them that can keep a referees' seminar occupied for three hours covering only two pages of the book. Such seminars, organized by local associations around the world, are another modern development and one that has done much to raise the standard of refereeing to its present high level.

In this chapter we discuss just a few of the rules which seem to cause most problems to spectators.

One difficulty that arises for television viewers (although it causes no trouble to other spectators) is the definition of 'top of the table' and 'bottom of the table'. It has always been the case that the end of the table where the black is spotted is the top. Since many discussions and commentaries frequently refer to the top of the table it can be confusing to television viewers because the main television cameras are always sited at the black spot end, with the result that on the television screen the top of the table is always at the *bottom* of the screen. The cameras will always take this position because all the action and the big breaks take place around the black spot and we will always have this slight confusion when watching snooker on television. The easy way to remember which side is 'up' is to bear in mind that the black spot end is the top of the table.

A question which is often asked is: 'When does the game begin? Is it necessary to strike a red first?' This is nicely answered by considering a problem frequently set in referees' examinations: 'Player A starts the frame but he is confused and he uses the yellow ball as a cue ball instead of the white. What is the penalty?' Now, the aspiring referee should know that under Snooker Rule 13(1) it is a foul stroke to use any other ball as the cue ball and the penalty for this is 7 points. *But* under General Rule 3(H) the game does not commence until the striker's cue ball has been finally placed on the table and struck with the tip of the cue. So the answer is that to use the yellow in this case is no foul because the game has not begun. It follows that once the cue ball has been placed on the table and struck with the tip of the cue the game is under way and all the rules apply. So if the striker moves the cue ball by only an inch or two, that is a foul stroke. He does not get another go just because he has failed to make contact with any red. If the first player has failed to hit any red his opponent does not put the cue ball back in the 'D' but plays from where the white lies (General Rule 13).

Two balls must not be pocketed in one stroke (except reds or the ball 'on' and the nominated ball where the player has a 'free ball') says Snooker Rule 8. This rule gives rise to many 'trick' questions and some serious issues during play. For example, the maximum break that can be made is 147 (or 155 in freak circumstances); but what is the smallest possible break that can be made, clearing the table? Logically, it might be thought, 72 – 15 reds, each with the lowest value colour, the yellow, plus all the colours. But remember Rule 8. All reds can (in theory) be potted in one shot so the answer to this puzzler is 15 reds (in one go!), plus one yellow, plus the colours (27), giving a total of 44.

Still keeping Rule 8 in mind, we must refer to Rule 10 which provides that if a player is snookered after a foul shot he may nominate any ball (commonly called a free ball). In these circumstances Rule 8 permits him to pot both the ball 'on' (where he is snookered) and the free ball in one shot. Time and again good players show an ignorance of this part of Rule 10 when faced with this position. For example, blue, the ball 'on', is over a pocket but between it and the cue ball sits the pink, fully snookering the blue. The black is at the other end of the table in an unpottable position. How can the player profit from the free ball? He cannot pot blue because he is snookered; he cannot pot pink alone because the blue blocks the pocket. The black is of no use to him. If the player doesn't know the rule that he can pot both balls, he cannot play what is virtually the only correct shot – to pot both the blue and the pink by a 'plant' so that he scores his 5 points and has the pink nicely re-spotted so that he can clear up. He can also, by means of the pink, knock the blue in and leave the pink on the lip of the pocket if that makes better positional sense. He can't do either in ignorance, and games have been thrown away by the player making what he thought was the only shot permitted, a safety shot. He is not permitted to roll up behind the pink (the free ball) because Snooker Rule 10 forbids the snooker behind a nominated ball – except where only pink and black remain on the table.

In all other circumstances it is a foul to pot two balls in the same stroke. An interesting example of a clearly foul stroke of this kind arose in the semi-final of the Pontins Open in 1975. Patsy Fagan (then still an amateur) was playing Ray Reardon, and in the last frame Fagan looked certain to be beaten as he needed a snooker and only pink and black remained on the table. The pink was in the jaws of a top pocket and any contact on it would pot the pink, ending the game. The match was of desperate importance to Fagan and he studied his hopeless position. His cue ball was in a dead straight line with the pink. At last Fagan got down to the shot, potted the pink and ran the cue ball through so that it too went into the pocket: a foul shot, costing Patsy six points. Ray assumed that in making this shot Patsy was conceding the frame and amid the applause he went to shake Fagan's hand in the usual way. Patsy shook his head and indicated to the referee and to Reardon that the pink, having been potted by a foul stroke, should be re-spotted. Although Fagan now needed two snookers, at least the game was still alive and he had a chance, however remote, of obtaining the two snookers and winning a very valuable match. The pink was re-spotted, the game continued and Patsy did not get his two snookers. But if he had obtained the required snookers and won the last frame, he would have done so as the result of a foul stroke which, at the time, drew no complaint from Ray Reardon or the referee. It seems clear that the referee should have awarded Ray Reardon 6 points and replaced the balls, leaving Patsy the same hopeless position – and no means of escape. It would obviously have been unjust for Patsy to win the match as a result of this inspired but unlawful shot.

One of the most dramatic actions a referee can take is sometimes seen in a match where a player has failed to hit his object ball, thereby making a foul stroke. The referee, without comment, may pick the cue ball up from where it lies, place it in its original position and tell the offending player to take the shot again. This usually occurs when the striker was snookered in the first place, and replacing the cue ball means that he's likely to foul again. This is nearly always a controversial action and it is one of the toughest decisions a referee must

Ray Reardon. Photo: Dave Muscroft.

face. Most spectators nod sagely and say, 'He's replaced the cue ball because it was a deliberate miss by the striker.' It is true that in these situations it probably was a deliberate miss – the striker would rather forfeit a few points than risk moving the object ball to a position where his opponent could pot it and clear the table. When he is snookered and makes his 'attempt' to hit the ball using two or three cushions, it is tremendously difficult to say that the miss was deliberate. But the rule that allows the referee to replace the white and tell the player to have another try says nothing about the miss being 'deliberate'.

The referee need not decide that it was a deliberate miss. An Official Decision covers the point: 'If the striker makes a miss, the referee can order him to replay the stroke, penalizing him the requisite forfeit for each miss . . .' The word 'deliberate' is nowhere mentioned. Five or six years ago such 'professional fouls' were being played with blatant impunity and few referees had the nerve to replace the cue ball. Today, because of the importance of the tournaments and the higher standard of refereeing, the action is taken more often by the better referees but it is probably true to say that players still get away with the deliberate miss more often than they are caught for it.

Snooker Rule 12 provides that if a player commits a foul shot, his opponent can ask him to play again. This rule was developed by the professional players and until fairly recent times was called 'the professional rule'. It is a very sensible and useful rule because there are many occasions when the forfeit of points would be a small price to pay if the opponent were obliged to take the next shot from a position fraught with dangers. So the opponent has a look at the table, decides that he can't pot anything or play a good safety shot (and if he can't, he reasons, the other player can't either), and asks the other player to play again, hoping that he will leave him something more attractive on the next shot. It should be borne in mind that a player need not be snookered before he asks his opponent to play again, but can ask him after any foul shot, regardless of the position of the balls. As television viewers will have noticed, the 'request' to play again can be almost imperceptible. Sometimes the player will say, 'Yes, please, John,' but often a mere flicker of the eyes or inclination of the head is enough to communicate the message – the position is, after all, quite obvious to the other player. In ordinary club or league matches it is a good idea to beware the man who volunteers to play again: he might simply be trying to be helpful, but more likely he's seen something that you won't notice if you don't take your time.

One aspect of play that has raised many questions in recent years is the amount of time a player can hesitate before he plays his shot. In the professional ranks and among the top amateurs there are players who are notorious for the deliberation they put into each shot: is there a rule about it? There is an Official Decision which provides that if the referee considers that a player is taking an abnormal amount of time over his stroke, with the intention of upsetting his opponent, the referee should warn him that he runs the risk of being disqualified if he pursues these tactics. No guidance is given as to how much time is 'abnormal'. There is little evidence within the game at any level that this power is often exercised by referees. The words 'with the intention of upsetting his opponent' make the offence very much more difficult to pin down – rather like the law in certain countries which declares adultery to be a capital offence but requires six eye-witnesses as proof of its contravention. There is no rule saying that a player has one minute or two or three to consider each shot. Referees must apply common sense. Thus, in a World Championship semi-final, where the last frame is at a critical stage, the referee may allow a player to think about a shot long enough for the television audience to go and make a cup of tea and a sandwich without missing much. When a player of that class does play his shot it is usually well worked out and well executed. No one much minds the long wait. But in a local league match where the team is not going to rise above tenth place in the third division and the players, for all their delay, play mundane shots, it is unlikely that the referee would allow them the time taken by the top professionals. There is the practical aspect – the club in which the league match is played usually closes at 11pm and the players cannot stay all night.

One of London's leading amateur players for over forty years, Dickie Laws of Hammersmith, is famous for his slow and deliberate play. He never accepted that there was any practical aspect to the matter; 'I'm here to win,' he would say, 'and there's nothing in the rules of snooker that says my match has to finish before the bar closes.' Time meant nothing to him and he would continue to play any frame where only the last few colours were left and he needed 50 points to win. He was capable of getting them, too, but his indomitable attitude and the time he took in considering each shot meant that he often did not finish a match in one evening. He and his bemused opponent would be turned out of the club at closing time with the scores at 3-3 and arrangements to be made for playing the deciding frame at a future date. Dickie Laws is one of the all-time greats of amateur snooker but referees and officials with homes to go to are pleased that he is unique!

Spectators are often confused about the re-spotting of the coloured balls when their own positions are occupied. The rule (Snooker Rule 7) is that the ball must be placed on the highest available spot. Thus if the black spot is free and a yellow has been pocketed but will not go back on its rightful spot, it must go on the black spot and, failing that, the pink spot, and so on. If all spots are occupied, any ball that is potted is placed as near as possible to its own spot in a direct line to the nearest point on the top cushion. In the case of the pink and black, should that direct line be obstructed by other balls, they are then spotted as near as possible to their own spots in a direct line to the *bottom* cushion.

A re-spotted colour (on its own spot or in another position) must never be spotted so that it touches another ball, and it is important for players to consider where the colour they are about to pot will be re-spotted. Many a possible big break has come to an end by the re-spot of the colour, in a position unforeseen by the player, snookering him. It is also Rule 7 which states unequivocally, 'reds are never replaced.' This causes much debate about unfair advantage from a foul stroke. Suppose that a player is 33 points behind on the last red. He can still win the frame by potting that red and the black or the pink. Even if he takes blue he can tie the frame. His opponent is in play, pots the red and goes in-off.

Doyen of amateur players Dickie Laws (right) with Hammersmith team mate John Pike. Photo: John Carty.

Foul stroke, 4 points to 'our' player. He is now 'only' 29 points behind, but he can't win without a snooker because the value of the colours left is just 27. He is at a grave disadvantage as a result of his opponent's foul stroke. To make the case even worse: suppose that the opponent is potting a simple straight red at slow pace into the corner pocket. He miscues and just touches the cue ball – a foul. Realizing what he has done and knowing that he is leaving a perfect red for his opponent, he cues through and pots the red. He may as well be hung for a sheep as a lamb: the penalty is still 4 points. His action in potting the red on the second strike may be swift, instinctive, but he can't leave such a position for his opponent. This is a clear deliberate foul and yet the rule says that a red is never replaced. What can the referee do? In this position the bravest and most senior referees say that they would disregard Rule 7 and put the red back where it was after the original foul, i.e. sitting in a direct line to the pocket.

What if the ball is played into a pocket at high speed, bounces out on to the cushion rail and rolls along it into the opposite pocket? A good shot, as viewers of the Jameson International semi-final between Dennis Taylor and Dave Martin will recall. Dennis played just that shot and although it is a fluke, they all count. Any ball which is forced off the table is out of play and it's a foul shot, but if it ends up in the pocket that is not 'off the table'. This shot is not quite as surprising as it seems. Although it is not seen frequently, it is almost certain that the ball will go across into the other pocket, first because of the force which made it come out and second because there is a line along the cushion rail between the wood and the rubber of the cushion which acts as a track and of course leads the ball to the opposite pocket. In most cases such a forced shot ends with the ball on the floor, but if it goes on the cushion rail it is more likely to pot in the opposite corner than to sit on the rail. If it does stop on the cushion rail, that is a foul because the ball is then 'off the table'.

There are one or two rules that don't often come into view in televized snooker but which make life interesting for referees in other matches. General Rule 10 provides that the non-striker shall avoid standing or moving in the striker's line of sight. He should sit or stand at a fair distance from the table. This is easily done in the excellent conditions of televized snooker (though occasionally a player can be seen indicating to the referee that he would like his opponent to move out of the way before he plays his shot). In ordinary club conditions, however, it is not quite so easy because there simply isn't the space to get far out of the way. Some players – thankfully few – stand on the line of sight, move about, light their cigarettes or blow their nose, and always at the critical moment. It takes a brave referee to tell this sort of player to behave. The worst offenders (usually when they are losing) will react to any warning from the referee by vehemently arguing the point for as long as possible and this may do more harm to the innocent opponent than the initial offence.

It is comforting that such players are few; that snooker at every level is generally played in an atmosphere of sportsmanship and goodwill; that there is General Rule 15 which provides that 'for refusing to continue the game when called upon by the referee to do so, or for conduct which, in the opinion of the referee, is wilfully or persistently unfair, a player shall lose the game and is liable to be disqualified for any future competition held under the control of the B&SCC or its affiliated associations'. Within the amateur game this drastic action is taken less than once in five years. What other sport can boast that?

Try this sample of questions taken from a typical 'C' grade referees' examination. The answers are given below.

1. Where should the pink and the first red be placed at the start of the game?
2. The brown and blue are pocketed in the same stroke and only the yellow spot is vacant. Where are the two balls placed?
3. Define a push shot.
4. What is the procedure if a player is 'angled' after a foul?
5. Yellow is the ball 'on'. A player has a free ball and nominates green. He misses the green and hits the yellow. Has he committed a foul?
6. After a foul stroke, the player nominates black as his 'free ball', red being the ball 'on'. He goes in-off black. What is the penalty, 4 or 7 points?
7. A player pockets a red and with his next stroke plays at another red. What is the penalty?
8. When has a player a 'free ball'?
9. When should a referee state, 'Touching ball'?
10. Should the referee award a 'free ball' immediately or on appeal by the player?

Answers
1. The pink should be on its own spot and the first red should be placed in a position directly behind the pink in a straight line 'up' the table, as near to pink as possible without touching it.
2. The highest-value ball (blue) is placed upon the yellow spot and the brown is placed as near as possible to its own spot 'up' the table without touching another ball.
3. A push shot occurs when a player strikes the cue ball at the same time as the cue ball strikes the object ball, and also when the tip of the cue remains in contact with the cue ball after it has commenced its forward motion.
4. If the player is 'angled' on all balls 'on', he can elect to play from the 'D' if he wishes.
5. Yes.
6. 4 points.
7. 7 points.
8. When he is prevented from hitting the ball(s) 'on' by a ball or balls not 'on'.
9. When the cue ball is touching a red, or is touching a colour after a red has been potted.
10. Immediately.

7

The turning point

Nowhere in the rules of snooker does it say, 'The player's heart shall be broken at regular intervals', yet every player knows, as surely as pink follows blue, that the game will torture and mock him just as it will gratify and reward him. There is something in the nature of the game – perhaps it is in all games – that always makes the defeats outweigh the victories, that makes a missed pot ten times more punishing than a successful pot is rewarding. The balance of good and bad is not equal. There is a psychological factor which will ensure that a missed black off the spot will replay itself a hundred times in the player's mind while his best shot of the week is somehow never recalled to mind with the same dramatic clarity.

The best way for any player to enjoy the game is for him to have a four-frame lead and score a nice 50 break or so in the early stages of each frame. There is nothing in the world so comforting as the sort of frame where one cannot put a foot wrong and the opponent takes no advantage of the few errors made. Even in a local club match that is the sort of game that sets a 30-break player thinking, 'Cliff Thorburn did it, why not me?' And somewhere the fates hear his delusions of grandeur and decree that for the next six weeks he will be unable to pot a straight blue off its spot.

In snooker, as in other walks of life, that's called *hubris*. No one is exempt from its effects. For a time the fates will smile on a Reardon, a Griffiths or a Davis and everything will go right for them. But even those who bask in the sunshine of great talent and good fortune cannot be sure that the sun will shine tomorrow. In the midst of their greatest successes they can still lose to an unknown amateur with bent knees and a corkscrew cue action in a working-men's club in Cumbria. It would be a dull world if every match result could be predicted in advance, if every player achieved his four-frame lead and progressed unruffled to the final and the first prize. Many games do take their expected course, favourites beat outsiders more often than not, but thankfully from the point of view of the spectators, the sport itself and, in the long run, the players, the long hand of *hubris* sometimes reaches out and changes the shape of a game.

In this chapter we look at a few great matches of the year, those matches which did not meander on to a foregone conclusion but which contained a turning point – a stage at which the wheel of fortune stopped, and suddenly started to turn the other way.

Steve Davis *v* Pierrie Mans
(Benson & Hedges Masters 1981)

For the first big tournament of 1981, the Benson & Hedges Masters at Wembley Conference Centre, London, the experts, the bookmakers and the fates were all on the side of Steve Davis, who had won three tournaments in 1980, the most recent being the Coral UK Championship, his biggest win to that date. His first match of the tournament was against South African Pierrie Mans, one of the most fluent potters in the world but a player who had not

Pierrie Mans. Photo: Dave Muscroft.

THE TURNING POINT

maintained the devastating form of his best year, 1978. Steve was odds-on favourite to win this match and Pierrie was 66-1 in the betting to win the title. On his arrival from South Africa, the first thing that Pierric saw in the newspapers was a reference to himself as 'a no-hoper from South Africa'. The normally genial and placid Pierrie was furious at this description: 'I didn't come 7,000 miles to be a no-hoper,' he growled.

The match opened as expected. Steve won the first frame easily. Pierrie won the next. No problems for the young Londoner – in the third frame he regained his lead with a 91 break. But then the Mans of old took charge. It is a feature of Pierrie's game that his reliance on extraordinary potting and his unique positional requirements make a mess of the table for his opponent. When he eventually comes to the end of a break, nothing is as it should be. The position of the balls on the table looks like the midway stage of a game between friends who couldn't make a 20 break between them. This unsettles the more ordered professional and he finds few opportunities to score or to work the game back into a pattern that suits him. For these three frames Pierrie kept his head down and the typical Mans pots went in, leaving the young superstar frustrated and adrift. Although Steve pulled one frame back with a 54 break he could not assert himself on the game and Pierrie won a startling 5-3 victory.

Main picture: Fred Davis. Inset: Kirk Stevens. Photos: Dave Muscroft.

Fred Davis v Kirk Stevens
(Benson & Hedges Masters 1981)

When these two were drawn to play together, the Canadian whizz-kid was expected to out-pot the cagey veteran Fred Davis. In fact it was Fred who went in front, relying on all his cunning and safety play, but it was a match in which most observers thought it only a matter of time before Kirk, with his greater stamina, would wear out the older man and pot him into the ground.

The question was whether Kirk's patience would give out before Fred's legs did. The young Canadian kept in the match and capably handled the veteran's tactics, eventually squaring the match at 4-4. Now the tide was running in Kirk's favour, here was the triumph of youth over experience. And so it seemed, as Kirk established a lead of 59 points to 4 in the final frame. He only needed a few more balls to complete the match and the balls were in position for him to do so.

Kirk wavered in deciding which red to play, made up his mind then changed it, and finally went for a reasonably potable red into the middle pocket which just nicked the jaw and rolled away. Fred was back in the match – and Kirk never had another chance.

Alex Higgins v Cliff Thorburn
(Benson & Hedges Masters 1981)

On a rainy Saturday afternoon in January, Alex Higgins, suffering from stomach ache, faced World Champion Cliff Thorburn: not auspicious circumstances for even the inimitable Higgins to

Alex Higgins. Photo: Dave Muscroft.

snatch victory from the jaws of defeat. Thorburn was at his most clinical in building up a lead of four frames to one. Alex was clearly unhappy and seemed resigned to an early finish to the session. In his dressing room during the interval Alex had a ten minute nap, but on the resumption he lost the next frame to trail 5-1, with the Canadian needing only one more frame to go forward to the final.

It was a subdued Alex who won the next frame. With breaks of 40 and 34 he took the match score to 5-3 and the word went round the bars and foyers, where many of the spectators had drifted to watch racing on television. At the start of the next frame they were all back in their seats and a new wave of excitement was in the air. Alex felt it. He was 57 points behind in the ninth frame and, spurred on by the increasing buzz from the audience, he cleared the table with a break of 85. The fans were on their feet, baying for more. He was again behind in the tenth frame and Thorburn, niggled by the partisan audience which was so firmly on the side of Alex that it applauded Cliff's *errors*, lost his concentration. Alex won the frame to make the score 5-5.

In the last frame it was Cliff against Alex and a thousand fans. They had seen their support for Alex lift him from certain defeat to possible victory and they would not be quieted or denied their climax. Higgins visibly fed on the waves of emotion and rose to the cries of the audience. He fluked a red in the last frame – to thunderous applause – and went on to make a 77 break which won the match. Never had a match been so dramatically turned around. Never had so many people without a cue between them played such a large part in a game of snooker. It could only have happened to Alex. It was one of the clearest demonstrations of the extraordinary effect the Irish star has upon an audience. For those last three frames he was not only *theirs*, he was *them*.

Terry Griffiths *v* John Spencer (Benson & Hedges Masters 1981)

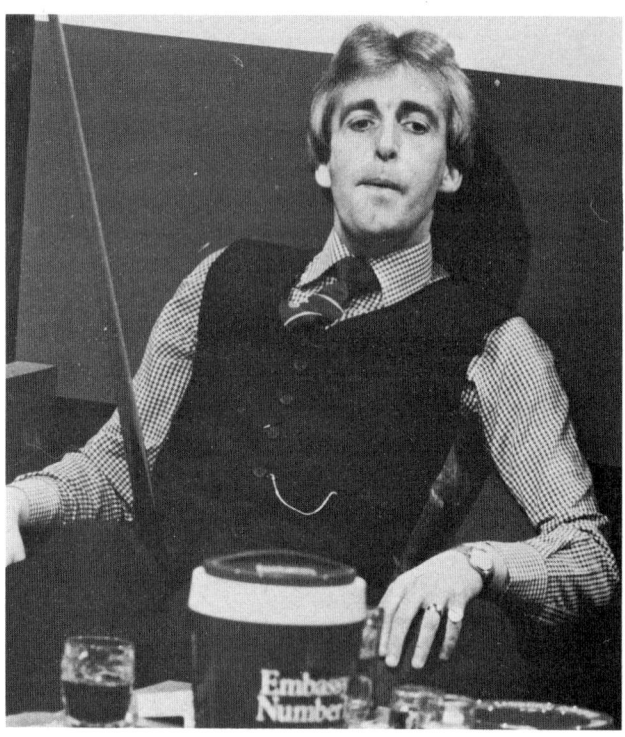

Terry Griffiths. Photo: Dave Muscroft.

This match of two former world champions had taken a slightly unexpected course as John Spencer, showing one of his returns to form, progressed nicely to a 5-2 lead. Although Spencer was not entirely happy with his game, he was comfortably coping with the off-form Griffiths and looked a likely candidate for a 6-2 win.

In the eighth frame Terry was as good as finished. He needed two snookers to stay in the match and on the evening's form this was a very unlikely prospect. But in one of those nightmare shots that every player dreads, John, in trying to escape from a snooker, struck the pink and left a free ball. This disastrous stroke cost John 10 points and enabled Terry to win the frame. In the next frame Terry played as it he didn't really believe he had a chance but 'gave it a go'. As an incredulous audience

THE TURNING POINT

watched, the tide turned in Terry's favour and he took the next three frames to win this marathon six-hour match at 1.30 a.m.

1981 was the year in which the English professional players got their own championship for the first time. This had been an obvious gap in the calendar, but as always, it could not be filled without a sponsor. In March 1981 the first John Courage English Professional Championship was played at Haden Hill Leisure Centre near Birmingham. It provided an interesting championship, being the first time that a major event had taken place in England without familiar names like Reardon, Griffiths and Higgins. This helped to concentrate the minds of the players and also asserted that despite the modern-day rise of the Welsh, the Irish and the Canadians, England still produces some very talented players. Although the championship was not shown on television the promotion was a success and it was won, as almost everything at that time was, by Steve Davis.

John Dunning v David Taylor
(John Courage English 1981)

John Dunning. Photo: Dave Muscroft.

John Dunning, of Gildersome in Yorkshire, has been a professional for over ten years but until the latter part of 1980 he was the forgotten man of tournament snooker. He had defeated Eddie Charlton in the 1974 world championship but otherwise had enjoyed little success. He had concentrated on his table-making and repairs business and he had earned a lot more money from making tables than he ever had from playing on them. The ratings system and the preponderance of 'invitation' tournaments had not helped his career and he observed with typical Yorkshire bluntness, 'I only get into the tournaments they can't keep me out of.'

David Taylor had also had less than his share of success but he had kept himself in tournaments and from about 1978 things had started to go well for him and he was now a world-rated player and number 2 seed in this championship.

David, in this match, was considered to be a runaway favourite – but John Dunning had his own ideas. He shook Taylor and the audience by taking a 3-0 lead. Taylor, with vast reserves of competitive experience, set to work and with the scores at 4-4 he could confidently feel that he had overcome the challenge of the Yorkshireman. Dunning, however, had not run out of steam and he again took the lead, making breaks of 48, 70, 63 and 39, showing an aggressive confidence that few, if any, of the audience had seen before.

David Taylor, now fighting to save his skin, levelled the match at eight frames each and breathed a sigh of relief as he made his mark in the last frame with a 44 break. It was not enough to keep the Yorkshire terrier down, however. With great determination and rock-steady play, John forced the frame to the colours and potted them all to win a black-ball game: a triumph for true grit.

Steve Davis v Tony Meo
(John Courage English 1981)

The final of the championship brought together two of the most exciting players in England, both of whom had earned their places in the final with good wins. Tony, especially in his match against Willie Thorne, had had the toughest path but Steve, in beating John Spencer 9-7, had needed all his skills to come through.

The turning point in the final came quite early in the match, but it was a crucial point. Tony Meo had started confidently and was potting all the long balls with more consistency than Steve. The Romford fans, that group of supporters who follow Steve to all his matches and have received more publicity and comment than any other fans in snooker, had settled down in great confidence and high spirits to

Tony Meo. Photo: Dave Muscroft.

watch their boy bring another title home. But as Tony forged ahead, the exuberant Romford group became ever quieter and for almost an hour nothing was heard of their calls of support – comments of obscure provenance which in the last few years have added a new vocabulary to the argot of snooker. They sat still and watched as Steve, undoubtedly shaken by his inability to get into the game, went 2-1 down, with Tony only requiring a simple yellow to leave Steve needing snookers.

Steve's complexion was two shades whiter than normal and the faces of the Romford fans were as white as the knuckles that gripped the seats in front of them. Steve Davis about to go 3-1 down! It wasn't allowed! Tony knew the importance of the yellow, an easy shot that he could hardly miss. Perhaps it was the pressure, the haste to confirm that he was 3-1 up on Steve Davis, that caused him to rush the pot and miss. Steve, scarcely believing that he was back in this frame, quickly wrapped it up and went on to a 9-3 win. The final score was convincing, and so was Steve as soon as he started breathing again, but who can say how it would have gone if Tony Meo had potted that one ball?

In the Embassy World Championship everything is magnified. There is so much more at stake and the matches have an importance beyond the world crown. There is always an influx of new qualifiers, sometimes a match where two players who have been professionals for four years realize that they have never before met in competitive play, and usually a few new faces from overseas. No one who plays at the Crucible can doubt that he is involved in the biggest tournament in snooker. When he comes out of those doors from the back-stage area and sees the television lights and the expectant audience, the nerves of any player, particularly if he is a newcomer, are severely tested. If the fates are ever-present in snooker, there is little doubt that at the Crucible they turn up early and take a ringside seat.

Graham Miles *v* Tony Knowles (Embassy World Championship 1981)

In this match Graham Miles of Birmingham, twice a winner of 'Pot Black' and a finalist in the 1974 World Championship, was thought to be a good but not insuperable test for Bolton's Tony Knowles,

Graham Miles. Photo: Dave Muscroft.

making his first appearance in the championship.

In recent years Graham has spent much time building up a business outside snooker to a turnover of more than one million pounds a year, and in the midst of this tycoonery it was not surprising that his snooker had suffered. He had, however, re-dedicated himself to the game and had clearly been practising to bring himself back to his high standards of old. The first evidence of this was in the Tolly Cobbold Classic at Ipswich, where he was a surprise winner in a tournament comprising himself, Alex Higgins, Kirk Stevens and Cliff Thorburn.

Knowles, a talented young player aching for a chance to show what he could do, had all the confidence he needed as he had convincingly beaten the world number 17, Jim Wych, on his way to the Crucible.

The greater experience of Miles was much in evidence as he took an early lead and always managed to keep in front. Tony was showing more flair and constantly threatened to come in with the really big breaks that can turn a match, but he was also showing 'first time nerves' and his few mistakes were costing him dearly. He levelled the scores at 5-5 and again at 6-6. Miles regained the lead but a superb break of 101 put Knowles back on level terms and he was like a greyhound in its trap as he waited for his next chance to get to the table.

At last Tony went in front 8-7 and in the next frame led by 38-0. It seemed clear that flair would now overcome experience. But Graham has flair too, and he won this frame to keep the match level. Although Miles then forced a lead of 9-8, he appeared to be weakening and Knowles still looked likely to prevail. Tony had the perfect chance when, in the next frame, Graham needed a snooker and Tony was nicely on the black, having potted the last red. Had he rolled the black into the pocket forgetting all else, Miles would have needed three snookers. Instead, obviously ruled by impetuosity or a desire to win in grand style, Knowles played a forcing shot on the black to give himself ideal position for the yellow – position he didn't need. He missed the black. He lost his lead. And he lost the match.

John Spencer v Ray Edmonds
(Embassy World Championship 1981)

Ray Edmonds, twice World Amateur Champion and twice a loser to John in the Northern English Championships, had never beaten Spencer in a match. In this encounter Ray was full of confidence while John was still not sure of his variable form or the reliability of his cue action. Midway through the

John Spencer (left) and Ray Edmonds. Photo: Dave Muscroft.

first session Edmonds took the lead and ended 5-4 in front. Spencer won the next three but Edmonds levelled again at 7-7. As the scores went to 9-7 in Spencer's favour, Ray bravely kept his spirits up and continued to show confidence. He is a player who tends to 'puff and blow', signalling his feelings to the audience whether things are going well or badly. The opponent can also read these signals and it is usually a big advantage to the player in the lead if he can see his man wilting. Ray refused to wilt and battled on until he scored a fortunate fluke on the pink.

With the scores level at 9-9, Ray felt that this time it would be different – this time he would beat the great John Spencer. There is, however, a pressure on the underdog about to have his day – a pressure to see the last black potted and the game over. For John Spencer there was no pressure of this sort. He was faced with defeat, to be sure, but it could come quickly or slowly: he'd seen it all before and for preference he'd rather it came slowly. He steadied down as Edmonds speeded up and his reward came with a 38 break and a more relaxed attitude. Edmonds, now in a lather of frustration, could make no impression and John won the match. Experience and calmness in that last frame gave

Spencer the result in a match which could so easily have gone the other way.

Dennis Taylor v Kirk Stevens
(Embassy World Championship 1981)

The Irish professional champion was a formidable test for the young Canadian but Kirk took early control of the match, showing many of his talents in addition to his obvious potting ability. He ended the first session 5-3 in front and Dennis who, like Fred Davis, finds that a chat relieves the tension, observed that he had never played so badly. Players who prefer to stay isolated during the course of a match can be disturbed by their opponent's small talk, but Kirk retained his concentration and his hold upon the match.

Stevens maintained his lead in the second session and Taylor, tough competitor that he is, could make little impression as the scores went to 8-6 in Kirk's favour. Then came the most controversial incident of the entire championship: Dennis went to pot a blue into the centre pocket. The balls were millimetres apart and it seemed clear that he would make a push stroke. Dennis went ahead with the shot and the referee, Jim Thorpe, called a foul for the push stroke. Dennis did not look aggrieved. Kirk went on to win the frame and make the score 9-6. In the next frame Dennis made a superb break of 135 to leave the overnight score 9-7.

Next day it was announced that the promotor, Mike Watterson, had relieved Jim Thorpe of further duty and had replaced him in this match with senior referee John Williams. The professional players themselves backed Jim's right to call the foul. The professional referees said nothing,

Kirk Stevens in play, watched by Dennis Taylor. Photo: Dave Muscroft.

THE TURNING POINT

presumably because Mike Watterson, although not a referee, was running the show and paying the wages. This one incident raised more controversy than any other single dispute in snooker and the debate will probably never die down.

Dennis Taylor's opinion of the shot, which he expressed to Jim Thorpe after the match was, 'Well, Jim, it was a fifty-fifty shot.' Later he said in more Irish fashion to John Hennessey of the *Daily Mail*, 'I felt that if Jim didn't call it, I wouldn't either. It was one of those shots. Definitely not a push – more of a shove!'

Mike Watterson's video tape gave him one answer, but the truth of the shot could be seen in Dennis Taylor's eyes. Every player who makes a foul which is not obvious to the referee (for example, scarcely touching another ball or striking the cue ball twice) reacts to what he has done – if he is aware that he has done it. The reaction may be caused by embarrassment, uncertainty or guilt, but the eyes tell the story. It is a reflex action that cannot be controlled, in the same way that the eyes express involuntary recognition of a familiar face. This reaction was the key to the entire plot of the classic thriller *The Thirty-nine Steps*, and to those of us who saw Dennis's eyes there isn't half as much mystery about this shot as there was in John Buchan's book!

The turning point of this match was not the controversial push shot but the fact that, behind the scenes in the bowels of the Crucible, Kirk Stevens was unable to use the players' practice table prior to the last session. The table was being used to record an item for television the next day and Kirk, deprived of his right to practice, was frustrated and bitterly hot-tempered when he came out for the final session. Had he expressed his feelings to the organizers and had a good row about it he may have fared better, but he bottled it up inside and it did his game no good.

Dennis started the session with a break of 60 to take the score to 9-8. Kirk won the next frame, but it was apparent that his composure was lacking. Dennis won the following one, with Kirk suffering some bad running of the balls, but a hard-worked break of 56 gave Kirk the next frame to maintain a lead of 11-9.

In the next frame Dennis made a fine 133 break, and as Kirk's spirits and concentration fell, Dennis's rose. Kirk still led by 11 frames to 10 but he was now fighting a rearguard action and everything about the game seemed to reflect this: his pots missed by fractions, his safety shots would unluckily stay in the open, his judgment was becoming erratic and his irritation all too obvious.

Dennis Taylor, despite his warm personality and reputation as a comedian, is a sturdy campaigner who has come up the hard way. As soon as he smelled the change of course, as soon as a few balls started going for him rather than against him, he was total concentration and he won the last three closely-fought frames for a resounding victory.

Steve Davis *v* Cliff Thorburn (Embassy World Championship 1981)

Cliff Thorburn. Photo: Dave Muscroft.

This was the best snooker match of the championship, and of recent years: the reigning champion, Cliff Thorburn, against the expected champion, Steve Davis; a match full of tension before either player reached the table. Thorburn had lost 6-0 to Davis in a challenge match at Romford two weeks before the championship and he was still seething at this result and the remarks of the gloating Romford fans in their own stronghold.

The first session was a hard battle with neither player giving anything – barely even acknowledging each other's presence in the same room. Confidence in the Davis camp was high as Steve ended the session leading 4-3, but Cliff was satisfied that there was nothing wrong with his game and that in time he would prevail.

In the middle of the second session, with the score standing at 6-4 to Steve, Cliff's game suddenly came together and for four frames he played some of the most meticulous snooker ever seen at Sheffield – or anywhere else. In those four frames he scored 347 points, while Steve scored 35, and 25 of those were in one frame. It was a superlative performance which had every person in the theatre wondering if this was the day the Davis bubble would burst. Steve, normally so much in control of his feelings, appeared to be suffering agonies and neither his manager Barry Hearn, his mother and father, nor any friend in the audience could take comfort from his deportment during these four frames. He slumped his head on his chest for minutes at a time, he examined his cue tip with eyes incapable of seeing anything, he alternated between rapid shallow breathing and deep somnambulistic breathing. He went red in the face. He went pale. He wiped his hands resignedly, neurotically. It was a shockingly uncharacteristic portrait of a man falling to pieces. At the end of this session, with Cliff now leading 8-6 overall, Steve's friends and family gathered around him, offering everything from love to pure oxygen. Steve winked.

The turning point of this match took place in private, inside Steve's head. At the start of the next session he bounced out into the arena looking as if he'd spent two weeks on a health farm rather than having just suffered the biggest thrashing in snooker. It was all water under the bridge. Gone and forgotten. He levelled the scores to 8-8, lost the next frame but recovered to 9-9 – all fiercely contested frames, with Cliff forcing Steve to produce only his very best.

At the end of this session it was the turn of Cliff Thorburn to show some untypical behaviour. With the scores at 11-10, Steve led 80 points to 23 and it was well past midnight. The pink and black were left on the table after Steve's shot. The pink had run into a position where it was not potable and, considering the frame score, hardly worth bothering to pot. However, snooker etiquette has it that even if there is a wide gap in the scores, the game is not over until the pink is potted (it being theoretically possible to gain an infinite number of snookers while two balls remain, and none at all when only the black is left). Steve, still at the table, turned to the approaching Thorburn and offered a handshake, obviously thinking that the session was over. Cliff sourly indicated that he wished to continue and refused the handshake. To the surprise of the audience he made to aim for the pink (a futile exercise in view of the frame score) and then got up from the shot and in an elaborate mockery of the Steve Davis habit, went over to his

Cliff Thorburn and Steve Davis shake hands after Steve's victory. Photo: Dave Muscroft.

chair, took a minute sip of water and returned to address the cue ball. He did not strike it but got up, turned to the nonplussed Davis and offered a frosty handshake. Cliff later apologized to Steve in private and to the public on television, but it was a remarkable episode that demonstrated more than anything the extremely high pressure of life at the top in snooker.

8

Such stuff as dreams are made on

Nothing in snooker is so much taken for granted as the cloth upon which the game is played. Good players may occasionally describe the table (and therefore the cloth) as 'fast' or 'slow' and are able to discuss personal preferences, makes of cloth or particular weights of cloth. No doubt the professional players have some expertise on the subject, but the opinions of lesser players are reminiscent of Scotsmen discussing whisky – everyone is an expert and has a favoured brand but only the barman, smiling as he listens to their judgments, knows that they are 'drinking the label' and not the brand they think.

Until recent years, brand names have played no large part in the marketing of billiard cloth. The billiard company that supplied or renovated a table would provide the cloth and it was seldom that the purchaser, usually a club secretary or billiard-hall owner, specified any requirements about the cloth other than that it should wear well and not be too expensive. Most of these customers would know that billiard cloth came from the West of England, Yorkshire or Belgium, but beyond that they knew little and relied on the judgment of their billiard supplier.

In recent times the name of one cloth has made its mark in the world of snooker. That name is Toptable, a cloth made by Hainsworth of Pudsey in Yorkshire, which has been used at one time or another in practically every major championship in the game. In producing a cloth which will be instantly recognizable around the world by its name alone, the aim is to do what Rolls-Royce did: achieve a standard of excellence and, having achieved it, maintain it on every single unit of production. There are rather fewer processes in producing a billiard cloth than there are in producing a Rolls-Royce motor car, but these processes are governed by the same requirements: skill, care, attention and refusal to accept any standard but the best, then work and more work.

As the table is set for the next major championship and the camera zooms in on the inviting sheen of a virgin cloth, we speculate as we await the arrival of the players. Will this become one of the few cloths on which a maximum break is made? How do they get it so flat and smooth?

Where does it come from? The answer to the first question is a mystery; to the second, a secret; but in this chapter we answer the last question by examining the making of a Toptable cloth from its origins in the Australian outback until it sits on a championship table, offering the results of the finest British craftsmanship to complement the skills of the world's finest players.

The cloth was born, like the phoenix, in fire. The old-established Hainsworth firm suffered a devastating fire at their mill some twenty-five years ago; they were under-insured and the losses almost closed them down. They had always concentrated on the production of wool for specialized outlets and even today their products are for such esoteric markets as regalia and uniforms, woollen parts used in the making of pianos (and there are dozens of such parts in a Steinway concert grand), and conveyor belts for biscuit factories. In putting the company back on its feet, the directors looked around for further areas of specialization and decided that there was room in the market for a high-quality billiard cloth.

The present chairman of the company, John Hainsworth, and his brother David, now managing director, came into the firm in 1955 and 1960 respectively and their success in producing triumph from disaster is shown in their bustling mills which now employ over 290 people. It was not easy to break into the billiard-cloth market, but Hainsworths were lucky in that Fred Ramsden of John Halliday and Co., one of the great names in billiard-cloth making, was nearing retirement age and wanted his specialized skills to live on after him. He sold his company to Hainsworth and he and John worked together to combine Fred's fifty years of experience with the bigger and more modern techniques of the Hainsworth mills.

'We set out to make the best,' John Hainsworth says. 'We moved mills around, bought new machines, designed others for ourselves – all sorts of traumatic things. I worked very closely with Fred, we spent hundreds of hours together, but through all that time and even up until today I have called him "Mr Ramsden" and he has called me "Mr John". He's in his mid-seventies now and still comes to the mill to see "his" cloth. He glows with pride when he sees a Toptable cloth and I know that if Fred Ramsden is satisfied with it then we can be proud of it.'

Getting the product right was the first half of the battle. The second was to persuade the conservative billiard trade that the new cloth was equal to or better then the cloth from their traditional sources. John and David are in the wool trade, not the billiard trade. Despite their expertise in marketing and management, they knew that they needed to penetrate the closed world of billiards and snooker if their cloth was to make its mark. They are the seventh generation of the family in the wool business, but the first generation in snooker. 'The skills we have are over a hundred years old – what we had done was to find a new application for those skills,' says John Hainsworth.

Just as the snooker boom of the seventies began to take off, Hainsworth engaged Randal Coe, a textile public-relations expert, to market the cloth. Sales increased dramatically and Toptable, a name devised by Randal Coe at three o'clock one morning, was established as the brand name in billiard cloth. 'We can't say what proportion of our business arises out of the big growth in snooker and what is attributable to our energetic sales and marketing,' says John Hainsworth. 'Although the Toptable name applies only to our full-sized billiard cloth and not to our productions for pool tables and so on, we can't even tell what our customers use it for. We'd love to know, for example, how much of our cloth is used for snooker and how much for pool. Once we've supplied the cloth it is for the specialist in the billiard trade to decide how he uses it and we don't know if some of it finds its way on to pool tables. We export to forty-two countries, a very important part of our business, and we can't keep track of what everyone does with the cloth.'

It is likely that the vast increase in snooker activity in recent years has helped the cloth establish itself in two ways: first, with so many new tables being built there is an obvious increase in the demand for cloth; and second, because the newer and younger image of the game comes from newer and younger thinking. With more go-ahead people in the billiard trade, the old idea that 'we buy from Mr X because we've always bought from Mr X' soon died and the old resistance to anything new has almost disappeared. But Randal Coe also played a large part: 'I thought the name Toptable conveyed the idea that in all good clubs there is one table that the best players always use and that seemed a proper connection. Then there is the idea of a top table at a dinner – we're selling something first-class and we wanted to associate the name with an image of class,' he said. Other manufacturers supplied their cloth by abbreviated code names signifying quality and weight and these codes were virtually meaningless to anyone but table fitters. By establishing a brand name for their cloth, Hainsworth have progressed to the position where the actual users, the buyers in the clubs, specify their cloth by name.

Their advertising has been entertaining as well as energetic. Their leading 'salesman' is Lord Hemsworth, a cartoon character invented by Randal Coe, who figures in their advertizing campaigns. In a bold stroke of publicity John Hainsworth bought the late Joe Davis's own table for £10,000 in a Sothebys auction in 1980 and offered it as a prize in a competition for Toptable buyers. The competition, naturally enough, involved devising a caption for a Lord Hemsworth cartoon and the campaign, which ran throughout 1980 and 1981, has been one of the most successful in snooker.

'We really do pride ourselves on our cloth', John Hainsworth says. 'There is no special Toptable supplied for championships – the cloth we put on a championship table is exactly the same as we supply to every customer.' That pride in doing something really well, in being a success story in the midst of an economic depression, is evident at every stage of the making of a cloth. In each stage of production hard-won skills are involved, and at a time when many crafts in the textile trade are dying out, the Hainsworth staff are busily applying these skills and passing them on to the next generation. 'We are aware that there's a risk of some skills simply being lost as the older people retire, but we combat that by training our staff to be multi-skilled,' John says. 'This not only covers us for any emergencies, but it also helps everyone to understand their part in the whole process.'

Within the mill the atmosphere is all efficiency, high concentration and good humour. And wherever John and David go they are 'Mr John' and 'Mr David' to the staff. 'Our people are highly specialized and could be lured away, but we have a very low turnover of staff,' John says. 'We like to think it's because they're happy here.'

The long road to the billiard table begins in Australia, where Hainsworth buyers select the sorts of wool they know will be required. Some fifteen varieties of wool make up the final mix and the skills of the buyers are crucial: 'There can be all sorts of things wrong with wool, and bad wool may not spin or it may not weave,' says John. 'Our people are looking for the best quality with no "burr" or "shiv" [varieties of dirt] in it. We rely on our people in Australia and consider them to be an important

Blended superfine Australian merino wool destined for Toptable.

Peter Hainsworth examines raw wool staple for the high quality needed to make a billiard cloth.

Completely modernized boiler house at the Hainsworth mill.

A view of the carding machine which combs the raw wool into strands of twistless thread.

part of our team.'

The supply is maintained by a British wool merchant, and woollen director Derrick Archer is the raw wool expert in Pudsey. Large quantities of the untreated wool, in massive 100-kilogram bales, are stored at the mill in a warehouse which is kept cool to allow the wool to 'rest'. The wool is washed to remove dirt and excess lanolin before it goes on to be blended. This is an art rather than a craft and the composition of the final blend is a trade secret. The wool is transported by air pressure along pipes and fed into an aluminium-walled room to be mixed. During the mixing, vegetable oil is added to improve the handling quality and later in the process this oil mixes with sodium carbonate to produce the soap used in washing the wool.

When the final blend is complete the wool, looking like puffs of cottonwool, is fed into the carding machines which comb it. These machines, covered in the soft white fluff, look like giant rollers caught in a snowstorm and the air around them is filled with fine wisps of fibre. Despite their strength and power, the operation of the machines, with their thousands of tiny 'teeth', is a gentle one and their precise setting is yet another crucial talent. The carding machines produce the wool in a flat form called a 'web'. This is fed into the final roller

The wool after processing into fine strands of twistless thread, or 'slubbing'.

it has withstood everything done to it, gaining strength each time and making the whole unlikely process work. On the mule the weak threads do occasionally break but the operator, who is walking up and down keeping an eye on 720 lines of fibre, can spot a break and he immediately moves in to repair it, working with such speed that the observer's eye cannot see what his hands are doing. Thus the line is rejoined, invisibly, and the mule rattles on.

Yarn measuring 35 miles – six times the height of Mount Everest – is needed to produce one length of cloth sufficient to cover a billiard table. Yarn is wound on to a beam for the warp threads and on to large cones for the weft thread (woven *across* the cloth).

The mule spinning yarn for billiard cloth.

to produce 'slubbing' – fine strands of twistless thread, looking for the first time like the sort of wool yarn we recognize, but it is weak and can be pulled apart without effort.

The next stage in the process is to put some strength into the wool, and this is done on the 'mule', a machine which takes dozens of individual lines of slubbing, pulls and twists them at high speed and leaves the strengthened yarn on bobbins. It is at this stage that the wonderful natural qualities of wool can be appreciated – this frail-looking stuff has been rolled, pulled, and pushed about, and yet

The next stage is weaving. The Hainsworth machines are their own design and specially built for them. They are called rapier looms because the weft thread is carried by a rapier, or blade, which shoots across the warp at an incredible speed. A second rapier, starting out from the other side of the warp meets it in the middle and carries the thread across the entire width of the fabric. As this stage is carried out, the material looks like a cloth for the first time although, of course, it is white.

The cloth is then examined for any flaws by holding it up to the light and minor repairs can be

The yarn is wound on to a beam for the warp threads prior to weaving the cloth.

Cone-winding the yarn before weaving the cloth.

Weaving billiard cloth on Hainsworth special rapier looms.

made at this stage if required. Having passed inspection, the cloth moves on to be washed.

After washing, the cloth is taken to a strange machine which looks more like an instrument of torture than a wool processor. It is a box with large wooden clogs in its base, called the fulling stocks. The cloth is carefully fed into the box and the giant clogs pummel back and forth, softening the cloth.

The next stage is the milling machine, which shrinks the cloth. It is passed through a 'throat' which is adjustable to determine the amount of felting and shrinkage and again, although the machine looks medieval, it is a very precise instrument in the skilled hands of its operator. The milling process takes advantage of the natural 'felting' qualities of wool and gives it its 'body' and density. Millions of pounds' worth of research have failed to produce this natural 'felting' in any synthetic material.

Having been shrunk to the required proportions and density, the cloth is then 'teasel-raised' to finish its surface with the 'nap', the characteristic feature of a billiard cloth. This is done by putting the cloth through a roller on which are set hundreds of teasel heads. A teasel is a tall, prickly plant whose egg-shaped flower heads are covered with tiny resilient spikes; their excellence in raising the surface of the cloth in a trustworthy and uniform way has yet to be surpassed by any man-made material. The teasels are selected by Bill Aston and hand-set in the frames which make up the working surface of the roller. His experience and judgment ensure that the teasels are correctly matched and even. It is a satisfyingly natural process.

Once the nap has been raised, the cloth moves on to be dry-finished. This involves cutting the nap on the cloth to the required length and it is done in exactly the same way as a lawnmower cuts grass. The Toptable cloth is distinguished from others by its shorter, denser nap and this stage of the operation is of critical importance – especially as the length of cloth being processed now has a value of about £1,500!

When finished, the cloth is rotary-pressed and,

The cloth is dragged through a narrow-throated milling machine which subjects it to heat, moisture and pressure, shrinking its total area by up to one half.

Hand-setting the teasels which are used to brush or 'tease' the face of the fabric.

The cropping machine which cuts the nap to the exact length.

having been 'ironed' for the first time, it is boiled in deep tanks of water to make the nap permanent.

After boiling, the cloth is ready for dyeing, the only stage of the operation not carried out in the mill. When it comes back from the dyers it really looks like a billiard cloth and the broad green rolls take their place alongside the vibrant scarlets of soldiers' coatings and the brilliant reds and apple green of piano cloth.

The next stage is dry-teaseling, exactly the same process as before and with the same purpose. Once the nap has again been raised, the cloth goes through a dry press to give it its final ironing.

And so, at last, a roll of Hainsworth Toptable is brought forth for final inspection. The inspection is always carried out by John, Derrick Archer and works manager Dennis Barrett. The cloth is spread out on a billiard table and the experts pore over it. There is something of the air of a wine-tasting about their deliberations. Each one notices different things, each has personal preferences. It would be unusual to find anything wrong with the cloth at this stage, 'but there would be a full-scale enquiry all the way back through the process if we did find something,' John said.

Because the entire mill is geared to producing a cloth of one consistent standard, there are no wide variations in quality between one roll and the next, but John and Derrick discuss every facet of the cloth, appreciating qualities and characteristics hidden from the layman's eye. As the final product of all this care and attention is rolled up to be stored, the 'working' side of the cloth seems to glow like fine grass on the Yorkshire Dales offering its dew to the morning sun. The men of Hainsworth, directors and craftsmen, as they handle it carefully, lovingly, almost fondling it with a reluctance to take their hands away until the last moment – their pride glows too. And so it should.

SUCH STUFF AS DREAMS ARE MADE ON   61

The rolls of cloth are boiled for six hours to utilize the natural felting properties of wool and set the 'nap'.

Brushing and examination of the cloth.

The men behind the success of Toptable (left to right): Derrick Archer, David and John Hainsworth and Randal Coe.

All photos in this chapter by Barry Wilkinson unless otherwise stated.

Part of the despatch warehouse which sends Hainsworth cloth all over the world to forty-two different countries.

Can Reardon rule again?

'Don't tell me you've got a snooker story. There's only one story in professional snooker – Ray Reardon beat somebody – and that's not news.' So said the sports editor of a national newspaper in 1976 and in his own misguided way he summarized the complete and utter dominance of the game that Reardon had attained in those days.

Ray had won the world professional title for the first time in April 1970, beating John Pulman 37-33 in the final, but he held the title for only six months because the championship was staged again in November of that year in Australia and Ray lost to John Spencer, who went on to win the title.

Although Ray was a world champion, a noted player and a 'man of respect' he seemed an unlikely superstar. John Spencer had a livelier, more modern image and he was the darling of the fans and the newspapers, who dubbed him 'King John'. Spencer was one of the lads, a fact much appreciated by the inner circle of snooker supporters, while Reardon was an ex-policeman, a fact which some supporters did not appreciate and which caused them to hold back their adulation, perhaps fearing that he'd take down their particulars if they applauded too loudly. In those days it was a struggle for any man to establish himself in a full-time snooker career, and although by 1972 Ray was a 'good earner' his early days of hardship were not far behind him and he knew that one championship win would not keep him at the top of the tree. The danger that he could slip back into the ranks and be just another professional player was never far from his mind.

Ray was immensely lucky that his wife Sue – probably the most efficient wife in snooker – was able to play an active part in his early professional years, looking after the business side of his life. She posted advertizing circulars, dealt with his bookings and coped with the growing volume of fan mail with a warmth and attention to detail that not only allowed Ray to concentrate on his snooker but also constituted a great public-relations exercise for him. Promotors, agents and managers could trust Sue, and this businesslike and reliable handling of his affairs (quite unusual in snooker at that time) did as much as anything to tell the world that this was a professional man.

In 1972 the spotlight turned from Spencer and Reardon to Alex Higgins and the unpredictable young Irishman attracted more publicity from more sources than snooker had ever known. Not all of that publicity was good, not all of it pleased the older players, and even as early as 1973 Alex was being fined £250 by the WPBSA for alleged bad behaviour, turning up late at matches and, as Ted Corbett, then of the *Daily Mirror* put it, 'for being Alex Higgins'. But, like it or not, the publicity generated by Alex created a new awareness of snooker and it attracted promoters and public in increasing numbers to the benefit of all players.

Reardon, the professional man, played on. He was the man to fear in any tournament. No one minded playing Alex – 'He gives you so many chances' – but the players could see that Reardon had tightened and polished his game, which had been hard enough to beat anyway.

In the 1973 world final Reardon had the worst possible start, losing the first session 7-0 to Eddie Charlton. He came back to win the next three sessions, but by the eighth session the television lighting had been installed. Ray was most unhappy with its effects and couldn't see properly. In those days the professionals had not had much experience of playing under television lights and the technicians had even less experience of snooker. The result was that the lighting was very fierce and, of course, much more widely spread than the customary light shed by three 150-watt bulbs under a billiard-table shade. The heat from the lights would also dry out the table and when the television crews turned up for any final their lighting would completely alter the speed of the table. Even when the players could see the balls they couldn't do as much with them, but had to roll balls and play them under-strength because the table was so fast. Nowadays the television technicians have ironed out their problems and achieve a reasonable balance of light (in photographic terms the strength of television lighting has decreased by three full f-stops in the last five years). They also tend to install television lighting at the beginning of a tournament so that there is no great change in the conditions halfway through.

Photo: Dave Muscroft.

However, in that 1973 final Ray was not happy with the lighting and told the tournament director so. The lighting was cut down and Ray went on to take his second world title, beating Eddie by 38 frames to 32. The incident of the lights is very characteristic of Reardon. He is not a man to suffer imperfections gladly and his career has been littered with protests and complaints about poor tables, unsatisfactory conditions or inept referees. There was a period in snooker's growth when organizers thought they had done well enough to stage a tournament at all, and that players should overlook inconveniences like beer crates instead of seats, unlit scoreboards obscured by someone's coat, or tables that would not give a genuine result in the world marbles championship. In general, the players suffered in silence: they had all seen worse on the exhibition circuit and they were afraid that any complaint in a big tournament might lead to the sponsors withdrawing the following year or, just as bad, not extending an invitation to the complainant next time. Reardon would have none of that. Taking his example from Joe Davis (not a man to suffer defects gladly – or at all), Ray insisted on speaking up when things were not to his liking. On occasion this caused bitter rows – especially when, as in the Watneys Final in Leeds in 1975, he demanded the removal of the referee and marker following some confusion over the scores in his match with Alex Higgins. The referees in those days were non-professionals, working for virtually nothing, with no recognized means of redress, and it was thought to be unfair of Reardon to pick on them. The answer to that was to improve the quality of refereeing generally – not merely to offer referees sympathy.

Again, in 1976 Reardon's objections to referee Bill Timms in the final of the Embassy World Championship led to Timms withdrawing 'due to illness' during the final and being replaced by John Williams. In this same championship Reardon, who had played all his earlier matches at Middlesbrough, arrived for the final stage in Manchester and complained about the television lighting (which was bad) and the table (about which other players were unhappy but had made no official complaint). Reardon asserted that the table was not level and demanded that it be 'put right'.

This insistence on improved conditions caused bad feelings and resentment against Reardon, who stood unmoved and unwilling to accept less than the best. He made enemies, no doubt, but when professional players today consider the near-perfect conditions at the Crucible and other big championships, where the organizers have taken every possible factor and contingency into account,

Reardon with John Spencer. Photo: Dave Muscroft.

where they have a qualified table fitter in permanent attendance and spare cloth and cushions in reserve – do these players cast their minds back to those days of not so long ago and mutter, 'Thanks, Ray'? They probably don't, but they should.

But back to 1973, and Ray was on top of the world again. He was in constant demand and was one of the most popular British players to visit countries like Australia and South Africa. In 1974 he began to look invincible as he took the title for the third time, beating Graham Miles in the final without difficulty.

In 1975 the world championship was played in Australia and no one had any doubt as to who would win it. Eddie Charlton, who claims he can never play his best in England and was the best prospect to topple Reardon, reached the final and indeed looked certain to win the title. Ray took a lead of 19-17 but Eddie overcame this and, taking 8 frames in a row, led 28-23. Reardon put the pressure on Eddie, who was desperate to do well in front of his own countrymen, and in the third last frame of this epic match Ray led Eddie by 30 frames to 29. Eddie came back to level the match and after 60 frames the world crown depended on the outcome of the last frame. Ray's usual calm authority and a break of 62 gave him this last frame and the world title, depriving Eddie of what was probably the best chance in his life of becoming World Snooker Champion.

At this time probably only Alex Higgins and Eddie Charlton genuinely believed that they could beat Reardon. Everyone else, especially the lower-rated players who have to be beaten on the way to the final, were defeated before they lifted a cue against him. John Spencer, his friend and close rival, was starting to lose ground. He still had all that natural flair – more than Ray had – but John had a more carefree attitude to life and perhaps also to his game. In the many great matches these two played, Ray was emerging as the winner. The other professionals could fault his cue action, curse his luck, wish for the chance to play him – but when they did they lost. He did not do it all by being a better player than everyone else – technically he was in the same class as five other people – but he did it by playing better snooker. It is a truism of the game that the better you play, the more luck you have. Reardon is not a man to court Lady Luck by gambling but she shamelessly granted him her favours and he won many matches where anyone but Reardon, doing exactly what Reardon was doing, would have lost. He hypnotized opponents. They played shots they should not have played, would not have played – but they were up against 'The Man' and it affected them all. Nothing affected Reardon. No matter how they tied him up, he escaped; no matter how they potted, he would find a cruel trap for them and leave them snookered in three different directions; when he was behind he came back relentlessly and when he was in front he did not drop his guard for an instant. And the balls ran for him – whether by luck or cunningly concealed judgment, it was sometimes difficult to tell.

John Pulman, watching Ray beating a revived Fred Davis in the Pontins Professional final in 1976, in the last frame of a match Reardon had 'lost' at least twice, demanded to know to which god Reardon prayed. It was not, of course, all luck. Nor was it purely professional skill. The winning ingredient in Reardon was character. He had a determination and will to win unequalled since the heyday of Joe Davis. There was an authority about him that made him, even in the company of the other players, a man apart. He was hearty and congenial in their company – but he was Ray Reardon and there was always a cautious edge of respect in the attitude of the other players.

He made himself a 'star turn' on the exhibition circuit. He did the trick shots, he laughed louder than anyone in the room, he made sure that even in the most obscure club he played as well as he could. He was a genuine 'club man' and the committee would like him, honour him and invite him back for another show. He was a successful newspaper columnist (although rather more negative and acerbic than was good for him), a popular and natural performer on television chat shows. He was chairman of the Professional Snooker Association Ltd, a company formed to represent the top players at a time when the newer professionals were exerting

CAN REARDON RULE AGAIN?

Inset picture shows Reardon with Alex Higgins. Photos: Dave Muscroft.

their muscles in the official governing body, the WPBSA, and in this role he was a skilful and tough negotiator. Never a man to undervalue himself or his fellow professionals, he played a large part in negotiations with sponsors and television companies, ensuring that the top players were properly rewarded.

In 1977 Reardon's reign as champion came to an end when he was beaten 13-6 by John Spencer in the quarter-finals of the Embassy World Championship. Spencer, showing a grim resolve that had been too long missing from his game, went on to become World Champion for the third time, beating Cliff Thorburn in the final. Reardon had arrived at the Crucible as a heavy favourite and it was a brave man who would predict any other winner. Joe Davis himself predicted Thorburn as at least a finalist. But Reardon did not have the same sharpness that had kept him on top. He seemed disorientated, distanced from the action. The pressure of his high-earning, hard-working life may have taken its toll: too much time spent in television studios and on the road and not enough spent in practice. In 1978, however, the bookmakers still made Reardon favourite for the title and he came through for his sixth win, beating Pierrie Mans of South Africa in the final. The previous year had been a hiccup – the Reardon supremacy was now re-established. Or was it?

In the United Kingdom Championship in November of that year Reardon lost 9-6 to Willie Thorne of Leicester, a match in which Reardon had been 7–1-on favourite at the start. Then other major tournaments were won by others: Reardon was being beaten. In the 1979 Embassy World Championship he lost 13-8 to Dennis Taylor in the quarter-final. Taylor was just the sort of player who in the past could never produce his best against Reardon. A talented player who, like many others, seemed too much in awe of the great man to think clearly enough to beat him. But Reardon had been shown to be human, beatable, and Dennis Taylor played some of the best snooker of his life in this match. Dennis's confidence was so high that on some difficult shots he ignored the rest and played left-handed. He is possibly the best player in the world using both hands, but to play left-handed is a risky business, normally signifying a lack of fear or respect for the opponent. It was a sign of the times, of Reardon's myth beginning to fade. Here was a man who, a few years earlier, couldn't cope with Ray using his best hand now summarily disposing of him using left-handed shots! So Reardon tasted defeat, and in the circumstances it was a bitter taste.

Photo: Dave Muscroft.

When the 1979 United Kingdom Championship came around Reardon, no fan of 'short-sprint' matches, was unwilling to give up or alter a lucrative exhibition contract sponsored by General Motors and for the first time in his professional career did not take part in a major British Championship. He was, of course, still high in the ratings, still a top box-office draw, and no one would run a big tournament without inviting Ray Reardon – but he was no longer two frames in front before the match started. Once players realized that he could be beaten like anyone else, his defeats became more numerous. His game had not greatly altered, he had not become a 'bad' player, but the level of concentration and commitment that had kept him at his peak was apparently difficult to sustain and it was his clear thinking and appetite for the game that was most lacking in these lean times. He looked, too often, as if he was somewhere else.

In the period from May 1978 until February 1981, when he won the Woodpecker Welsh Professional Championship at Ebbw Vale, Reardon won no major individual titles. This period was marked by the rise of aggressive new players, whose influence on the game was wider than their results in matches alone. One of these was John Virgo, who not only said he feared no man but also played and spoke as if he meant it. His baleful views on the leading players of the day, widely reported in the press, ended some of the 'forelock-touching' that seemed to exist among the lower-rated players. Who but Virgo in the late seventies could describe Reardon and Spencer as 'yesterday's men'? Other young players like Thorne and Patsy Fagan did not become involved in the slanging matches, but in their play they were treating Reardon as just another player. The bubble of invincibility had burst and as the eighties dawned there were Doug Mountjoy, Steve Davis, Jimmy White and others gaining prominence, leading a very crowded professional scene and making it unlikely that the conditions in which Reardon had thrived, when a player could know intimately all the strengths and weaknesses of the available opposition, would ever return. Today there are too many players to allow this, they're too good – and they have no respect for their elders!

In 1980 Reardon's cue 'died' of old age and he suffered agonies trying to find a replacement. Until he finds a cue that he can trust as he did his lifelong partner, he is unlikely to command the heights again. In Glasgow in 1981, playing in the Scottish Masters, he lost to Jimmy White, and in interviews after the match Reardon said he would retire if he could play no better. The newspapers carried reports of this surprising statement, telling the world of his cue problems. The response proved that Ray has a special place in the hearts of snooker fans. He was deluged with offers of new cues, old cues, advice, sympathy and messages of support. His threat of retirement had never really been serious, but when he saw the response from the public he was touched and immediately assured them that they had not seen the last of him yet.

So can Reardon rule again? The word 'rule' describes better than any other what Reardon did at his peak. He did not just win; he was not just World Champion: he was, in his supremacy, majestic, and towered over others as surely as a monarch on a throne with the courtiers in their places below. It is unlikely that anyone will again dominate the game so thoroughly and for so long as Ray did – even if all the signs now exist that one young man in London is quickly showing that he could. Can Reardon win the world title again? The answer to that is a cautious 'yes'. Sue Reardon, who knows this man better than anyone, gave the reasons shortly after Ray lost the title last time, 'Of course he will win it again. He has too much skill, he is too much of a professional not to.'

And if he doesn't win? He has written his place in the history of snooker. He is assuredly one of the best match players the world has ever seen. His record will not easily be surpassed. Reardon showed an entire generation what must be done to play like a champion, to live like a champion. That will be his legacy. But even more, Reardon is a professional, and the term attaches to him with a special significance: his conduct, his bearing, his personality and character did more than those of any other man to raise the status of professional snooker players to the high level of public regard they enjoy today.

10

Wales: factory of champions

It is a land of legends, of music and poetry and tales of when times were; a land of culture where every village values its choir, its tenor or its man of vision, where rugby players become immortal before the age of forty, where prizefighters bring something of the mystery and elusiveness of Wales to the unpoetic world of fisticuffs; a land of hard labour, harsh poverty, of lush green valleys, forgiving hills, quiet places reflecting the soul of Wales. And everywhere are the scars of man – the refuse and the debris of an industrial past lie naked in the valleys, offending nature, contradicting the spirit of the country. But the debris signifies work – and there have been too many times under too many roofs when work was a luxury to be dreamed upon.

Yet the spirit and the soul of Wales survive. Something of that spirit came out of the mines, the steelworks and the shunting yards into the social clubs which offered companionship, a warm fire and a kind of civilized resort when the labours of the day were done. The nature of billiards and snooker attracted the men of Wales who needed some challenge other than the hewing of coal: men whose character made them seek the company of others, but whose puritanical upbringing could not allow them a night of ribald beer-swilling and the search for oblivion in the name of manliness and good fellowship.

Perhaps it is all accidental. Perhaps there is nothing to distinguish a Welsh snooker player from any other. Terry Griffiths may be a pedestrian workman earning his living at something he happens to do well. Perhaps – but the record books say otherwise. Wales is a small country, lacking in riches and adequate roads, but it has produced some of the greatest players of our age, and at every level, amateur and professional, it has been able to boast a disproportionate number of champions and fine players. Within the last eight years Wales has shown some signs of dominating snooker and today, in the snug bars and welcoming parlours, the new

Cliff Wilson. Photo: Dave Muscroft.

Ray Reardon. Photo: Dave Muscroft.

legends are being born. But now the stories are not of Jimmy Wilde, Gareth Edwards and Geraint Evans, but of Ray Reardon, Terry Griffiths and Doug Mountjoy.

It began with Ray Reardon and Cliff Wilson. Reardon today is by far the better-known player: he has been World Champion six times, captain of the Welsh professional team, winner of virtually every title in the game, television personality, star. But back in Tredegar in the 1950s it was Reardon and Wilson, and many of the observers of those days would claim, with some accuracy, that it was Wilson and Reardon. The two were equally matched. Cliff Wilson was the more spectacular player, surrounded by a group of raffish supporters who would meet any wager against their man. Reardon, even then, was the self-possessed, calm player we know today. His supporters were as devoted to him as were Wilson's, but they were considered to be a rather more respectable group.

The town of Tredegar had two working-men's institutes or clubs. Reardon was the favoured player of the 'bottom 'stute', as it was known, while Wilson was the star at the Lucania Billiards Hall at the top end of the town, known as the 'top 'stute'.

Terry Griffiths. Photo: Dave Muscroft.

Throughout the 1950s the rivalry between these two was a never-ending source of fascination to the local snooker community. There was much antagonism between the rival groups of supporters, but between the two players there was always great respect. Often when one of them was practising in his particular ''stute', the other could be found standing quietly in the shadows, just watching.

Although Ray Reardon won the Welsh Amateur Championship in every year from 1950 to 1954, Wales was only one region for the purposes of the All-England Championship and it produced only one qualifier. Wilson barred Reardon's path in two English championships, and on the occasions when Reardon did qualify he did not do himself justice in the final stages in London. In 1954 he moved to a new job in the Florence Colliery, Stoke-on-Trent, and the invisible chains that shackled him to Wilson were at last broken. In 1956 he reached the final of the All-England Championship, losing to Tommy Gordon 11-9.

In Tredegar, at least, the perpetual clashes of these titans had raised the interest in snooker to new levels. Throughout the principality other players tried to emulate their feats and the general standard of play rose a little.

As with everywhere else, not much happened in Welsh snooker in the 1960s. As with everywhere else, the fires were kept alight in amateur snooker and the first rumblings of rebirth and growth were felt in the amateur ranks at a time when the professional game was still comatose. There was, however, one significant occurrence in Welsh snooker in 1965. In that year the chairman and secretary of the Neath League in West Wales was elected as a delegate to the Welsh Control Council. His name was Mal Hendra, today the chairman of the Welsh Council, and there is little doubt that most of the development of snooker in Wales stemmed from this former shop-steward, Welsh snooker's own man of vision.

Hendra began to take a serious interest in the council in 1967. He was impatient with the hidebound ways of the old-guard councillors – and they were less than pleased with the brash ideas of this aggressive newcomer. But Mal had been carefully advised by E. G. Jones of Paglan, a schoolmaster and league secretary for more than twenty years, and Mal relied on his advice to 'be strong, but don't push' in his efforts to drag the Welsh Council, kicking and screaming, into the latter half of the twentieth century.

'When I first attended the council I was like a communist at a Conservative Party Conference,' Mal recalls. 'Half of them didn't understand what I was on about, the other half understood only too

John Parker and Mal Hendra at Mackworth Club, Neath, with the Prince of Wales Shield. Photo: John Carty.

Doug Mountjoy. Photo: Dave Muscroft.

well and they opposed just about every new idea. They did it very nicely. They would agree with me in discussion – then vote against me.'

The council went along in its accustomed way until, in 1971, at Mal's instigation, a competitions committee was formed with Mal as chairman. He had always known that the strength of Welsh snooker was in its players, and given the chance to organize these players he knew he had all the power he needed. He set about arranging tournaments, making sure that the players knew that in their council they had something which needed their support and which would repay their support in a practical way by giving them more tournaments. The international matches with England had recently started and these, with the possibility of a place in the Welsh team, provided the spur for all ambitious players.

'One thing that held us back was that the old Control Council did whatever the Billiards Association and Control Council said,' Mal recalls. 'We started to question that and now we do what we think is best for Wales. We're not afraid to tell the world governing body to get lost.' The finances of the old council depended heavily on subscription fees from leagues. There were about thirty leagues paying £5 per year each (recently increased to £10), and although some of these leagues had as many as sixty member clubs, their contribution was limited to one payment of £5 each year. Just as the Welsh Council resents interference from England, so too the leagues resent too much control from their own council. The leagues are fairly wealthy and fiercely independent, and the prospects of greater revenues from them were always remote. The council had no category of 'individual member' and so the players, who benefited most from the increased activity, could not be made to pay membership fees. However, they could be made to pay entry fees for competitions. As more and more competitions were launched, the council's income from this source rose to more than £1,000 a year.

'That's our main asset, compared with England,' says Mal Hendra. 'We run many more competitions and it keeps the players sharp. I would say that from February until the end of the season (June) a top-class Welsh player would be playing three nights a week in Welsh Council events alone.'

Since the international matches had begun in 1969 England had won the title each year. Scotland and Ireland took part from 1970 onwards, but the battle for supremacy was always between England and Wales. In 1974–5 Wales won the title for the first time. This was a period when everything started to go right for them. Mal Hendra points to two reasons for the dawning of success: 'The groundwork of the last few years was starting to pay off, and John Parker became Welsh secretary in 1974–5. I think a lot of our success was due to John's efforts as a businesslike secretary.'

John Parker of Aberdare, an established league player and pairs partner of Terry Griffiths, thinks that the biggest change was that, in the atmosphere created by Mal Hendra in the Welsh Council, they were now allowed to think commercially. 'Mal and I were both "players' men" – we knew what the players wanted and it cost us out of our own pockets to provide it. I believed that the snooker supporters would provide the finance and I think we showed that this was true.'

Their biggest venture was the promotion of the Wales v England match at Rhydecar Leisure Centre in 1976. 'Some of the older people on the council were reluctant to run the risks of a big promotion in a leisure centre, but we felt that the ordinary clubs which had been used in the past weren't suitable for such an important match,' said John Parker. In the event, John and Mal were proved right. The international match was played over two days and was their most successful venture up to that date. With tickets priced at a modest 75p, the arena was packed, Wales won and the council, after paying all expenses including those of the ten-man England party, made a profit of £800. Later that year they followed the same plan and staged the final rounds of the Welsh Amateur Championship at Hill's Cricket Club, Merthyr Tydfil. This promotion drew 2,000 spectators in four nights and on the final night many spectators had to be turned away. The promotion made a profit of £1,700. The Welsh Council was now financially secure.

In that 1976 championship the matches were of crucial importance because the winner was to join the 1975 champion, Terry Griffiths, as his country's representative in the World Amateur Snooker Championship in South Africa. In Wales today they still talk of the match in which Doug Mountjoy was helped on his way to South Africa by a fly! In his semi-final match against Dai Thomas, Doug was 6-5 down and in trouble. Dai needed only a simple green to put the game beyond Doug's reach, but he was disturbed by a fly buzzing around the table. He swatted it a few times but the fly was persistent and Dai would not complete his match with Doug until he had first won the skirmish with the fly. He chased it around the table, under the light and eventually pursued it all the way into the audience! On returning to the table his concentration had gone and he failed to pot the simple green. Doug went on to win the match and ultimately the title.

As a nation in its own right, Wales has the honour and the burden of sending two players to the World Amateur Snooker Championship every two years and to the World Amateur Billiards Championship in the intervening years. Since the World Snooker Championship had started in 1968 it had always been won by an Englishman and no Welshman had won the World Billiards since Horace Coles in 1935. In Johannesburg in 1976 Doug Mountjoy became the first Welshman to win the world amateur title. In 1978 Cliff Wilson repeated this feat in Malta, breaking the English stranglehold on the world title. However, in a bitterly opposed move in 1981 the Council abandoned billiards, failed to stage a national billiards championship and sent no representatives to the World Amateur Billiards Championship in Delhi in November.

Doug Mountjoy had long had ambitions to turn professional and he did so immediately upon winning the world title. Terry Griffiths, the other Welsh competitor in South Africa in 1976, had no such plans as he preferred the security of his life as it was. Terry won the English Snooker Championship for the second time in 1978 but it was the Welsh Championship which would determine whether he would represent Wales in Malta later that year. On the Thursday following his win in the English final, he played Steve Newbury of Neath in the Welsh Championship at Garnant and lost 4-0. It was a long time to wait for the next World Championship in Tasmania in 1980, and Terry decided to turn professional. He had been watching his friend Doug Mountjoy's progress in the professional game and there is no doubt that this influenced his decision. Since turning professional in 1976, Doug had won the Benson & Hedges Masters, BBC Television's 'Pot Black' tournament, and had been a close finalist in the UK Championship. He was doing very nicely as a professional and Terry decided that his future too lay in that direction.

While the Welsh were making their mark on the world scene, it was done at some cost. The Welsh Sports Council (which considers Welsh snooker to be one of its success stories) provided a grant for travel costs in addition to the annual grant of £1,200, but the Welsh Council, with an income not much greater than some English county associations, has to find the balance of the costs. In the 1980 championship in Tasmania the total cost to the Welsh was £3,500.

Relying on the political will of Mal Hendra and the business acumen of John Parker, the Welsh Council had provided a strong structure within which the players could concentrate on improving their skills and realizing their ambitions. It was more than a two-man enterprise, however, and many councillors made their contribution. Philip Walters, a Cardiff solicitor, was chairman of the council during its years of growth and proved to be a solid, steadying ally to the dynamism of Hendra. Keith Robinson of Cardiff also played a part, especially in the areas of sponsorship and publicity.

Since 1973 Wales has had an advantage over every other amateur association – its own television tournament. Harlech Television have produced an annual tournament for the top amateurs which has ensured that, unlike players in the rest of Britain, the amateur players of Wales are known to the public and have a chance to establish their personalities just as the professionals do. The players take part by invitation, but the system is flexible and ensures that all regions of Wales are represented. In the past the television company and the council were brought together through intermediaries and the council did not have direct control of the event. The aggressive policies of Mal Hendra soon put a stop to that and this tournament, and all other television coverage of Welsh snooker, is now negotiated direct between the council and the television company.

The new power of the Council is not exercised only in relation to televized tournaments. A few years ago a big professional match was set up between Ray Reardon and Doug Mountjoy at the Double Diamond Club, Caerphilly. The promotor

Photos: John Carty.

Steve Newbury.   *Keith Robinson.*

was of the opinion that a professional tournament was not the concern of the amateur ruling body and made no approach to the council for referees or any other assistance. The council made it known to him that they should have a part to play in this enterprise. The promotor disagreed. Mal Hendra and the council directed all their clubs and members not to support or publicize the promotion. Plans were made to picket the Double Diamond Club and even to stage an attractive match elsewhere in Caerphilly that night.

'It might seem an over-reaction,' says Mal Hendra, 'but we had to establish that we are the governing body of snooker in Wales and that it was our people's money that would support the tournament. We made it clear to our members that they were either with us or against us and they supported us. I will stop any promotor, Welsh or not, from coming into Wales and making money on the backs of Welsh people. They should give something back to the governing body of the game.'

The pickets were never used, but the Welsh supporters got the message and the tournament was a financial disaster.

'I had a phone call the next week from one of the organizers telling me that our action had cost them £7,000,' Hendra recalls, 'but if they'd come to us in the first place they could have had all the publicity and assistance from us for a fraction of that figure.'

Since that time the Woodpecker Welsh Professional Championship has become established and the professional promotors of that event always seek the assistance of the council. The same company also sponsors the Welsh Amateur Championship, so there are closer links than existed in the past.

'I don't believe we acted unreasonably,' says Mal

Pictured on the occasion of the 1981 Welsh Professional Championship are (left to right): promoter Ray Davis, Cliff Wilson, referee John Smyth, Ray Reardon and John Rudgard of Bulmers, the sponsors. Photo: John Carty.

Hendra. 'This is a small country and I don't accept that there should be any big difference between amateur and professional players. All the Welsh professionals were *made* by this council. Reardon was too early to have benefited in the same way, but all the others have had hundreds of pounds and hundreds of hours of amateur effort invested in them – and they don't forget that, whatever the promoters might say.'

This certainly seems to be true of the world of Welsh snooker. Both Doug Mountjoy and Terry Griffiths did shows for the benefit of the council when they first became professional players. When Terry won the Embassy World Championship in 1979 he came into the Mackworth Club in Neath on the following Monday, bringing the trophy with him. He stayed to talk to the youngsters and to sign autographs. No one had 'booked' him, no one had asked him. He just thought it would be a good idea. In the following week he travelled to Bridgend for the junior championship and refereed some of the matches. The professionals are still close to their amateur roots, most of them live in the same towns as before – but in bigger houses – and this provides an incentive for the younger players trying to make a name. They can see what Doug, Terry or Cliff have done, see the expensive cars they drive, hear of the exotic places they've been. And they can think, 'Why not me?'

In every valley, in every village, there is at least one table and usually more than one very competent player. There are snooker centres throughout Wales, each with ten or twelve tables in continuous use. Some of the centres, mainly operated by the Mackworth group which is an important sponsor of amateur snooker, are in villages with a population of 3,000 or less, places like Bryntirion or Ystradyglandais which do not appear in bold letters on any map. Yet these little villages, and those surrounding them, make a commercial success of a snooker centre which would be a grave risk in an English town with a population of 30,000. It is easy to say that they have nothing else to do. But that is not the whole answer. Many people with nothing else to do spend their leisure hours playing mediocre snooker. The Welsh do it differently. They produce winners, they produce champions. It may be that they have the example of their professionals to observe and follow at close quarters. It may be that snooker for many of them represents a road to fame and fortune which will not be easily found elsewhere in the valleys. It may be that every time they set foot outside Wales they feel that, no matter what the level of the match, they represent their country. All of these things play a part. But the obvious reason for their growth is that, in the organization of Welsh snooker, Mal Hendra and his colleagues in the Welsh Council have created a structure that produces winners the way Ford produces cars. Any player, whatever his or her age, knows that life for them is essentially simple – all they have to do is beat people. The structure will do the rest.

If they take advantage of all the opportunities they're given and play in the dozens of matches available to them, Welsh snooker players' skills will take them where only their dreams have gone before. From an obscure club in Llanelli to the championship of the world. A dream? Perhaps. But if a Welshman can't dream, who can? And it's not just a dream – Ray Reardon and Terry Griffiths did it, didn't they?

11

Dennis Taylor: laughing all the way to the bank

Another roar of laughter subsides. Dennis Taylor moves around the table to set up his next trick shot. He's smiling as he places the balls, but one eye is shrewdly watching the audience, sensing its mood, like a huckster in a market hoping no one will open the bag before they've paid their money. The next trick must be set up with great precision but the audience needs to be entertained, kept warm. Dennis lifts the triangle which will feature in this trick, examines the wood of which it is made, turns to the audience: 'I hope this trick will work, this looks a bit thick.' Fractional pause, voice from the audience, 'It's an *Irish* triangle Dennis!' He smiles, grateful for the expected but entirely unrehearsed heckle. 'No, I don't think so,' he says, studying it. 'Back home we make them square!' More laughter and applause and the show rolls on. The audience is startled by the accuracy and success of the tricks and captivated by the endless stream of jokes and gags that go with them. It is, surely, enough to expect a man to be able to play snooker so well as to be constantly rated in the world's top ten. When that man can also have an audience on its feet like a Bible Belt evangelist and tell jokes with the timing and impact of a professional comedian, he must be something special. Dennis Taylor is special. He made himself so.

He started to play snooker at the age of eleven in Gervin's Club, Coalisland, County Tyrone. For the first two years he was regularly beaten by his big brother Martin, five years his senior, but soon Dennis overtook Martin, and at the age of fourteen, having won two big local competitions on handicap, he could beat almost anyone in the area. He spent all his free time playing snooker and was always on the lookout for better players from whom he could learn something.

When he was seventeen Dennis moved to Darwen in Lancashire to live with an aunt, partly to look for work but also to improve his snooker. He found the work but he also found that the standard of snooker in England wasn't as high as he'd thought. He played for the Benarth Club in the East Lancashire league but was frustrated that the league matches only gave him one frame and many players treated the matches as a good night out rather than a serious contest. At eighteen he won the East Lancashire Senior Championship – a title he was to win four times in five years – and the British Boys' Billiards Championship, beating Dave Burgess, then of Portsmouth, now living in Croydon, in the final.

He was an acknowledged first-class player in the East Lancashire area and when, at the age of twenty, he achieved a 136 snooker break in a tournament in Blackpool, he made his name nationally. This break satisfied all the conditions for a world amateur record but, to Dennis's disappointment, it was not officially recognized as such.

The next step in Dennis's career was an unlikely

Photo: Dave Muscroft

Dennis with wife Pat, daughter Denise and friends from Gervin's Club, Coalisland, County Tyrone.
Photo: John Carty.

one and as good an 'Irish joke' as anything he was later to devise: the late Bill Cottier, chairman of the B&SCC and final selector of the England team, was not deterred by a slight formality like nationality and invited Dennis to play for England! Dennis was as surprised as anyone else by this invitation, but if he had refused it his snooker life might have been rather uncomfortable in the Lancashire area which Cottier ruled like Mayor Daley in Chicago. 'I accepted it because I thought it would do me good,' Dennis said diplomatically.

Dennis had settled in Blackburn, Lancashire, where he still lives, and at this time John Spencer was the biggest name in the area. Dennis learned a lot by playing and watching Spencer. They used to play in an exhibition series sponsored by the *Blackburn Evening Telegraph* and Dennis took over John's leading role in this when the latter turned professional. He accepted the position as manager of the Elite Snooker Club in Accrington, which was jointly owned by his friend Ben Clarkson, and from this background he took the speculative step of turning professional at the age of twenty-three.

In his first World Championship Dennis lost 9-8 to Cliff Thorburn on the final pink and felt that his nerves had got the better of him. Supported and encouraged by his wife, Pat, he decided to take the plunge and enter himself in the John Player International Tournament in Toronto. It was a big gamble, because if he didn't do well he couldn't possibly cover the expenses of the trip, and as a struggling young player he couldn't afford to lose hundreds of pounds. In the end he did very well, beating Alex Higgins in the semi-finals and narrowly losing to Cliff Thorburn in the final.

During the course of this tournament, in practice against Eddie Agha of Montreal, Dennis made a record snooker break of 349. Sounds Irish? What he did was to clear the table with a 103 in the first frame and on his break in the second he fluked a red and cleared the table making a break of 134. From Eddie's break in the next frame Dennis made a 112 break to record a total of 349 in continuous play.

Soon after his return to England, Dennis was invited to appear in the BBC television tournament 'Pot Black'. He was not the most obvious choice but Ted Lowe, who advises the BBC on the invitees, felt that this young man had something to offer. Dennis proved his credentials by reaching the final, losing to Graham Miles, and for a time Ted Lowe enjoyed a reputation as a clairvoyant as well as a snooker expert.

Harsh reality faced Dennis when the details of the next Word Championship became known. It was to be played in Australia and he had to pay his

DENNIS TAYLOR – LAUGHING ALL THE WAY TO THE BANK

own expenses. It was a formidable hurdle, but his friend Frank Harrop showed him how to do it: they wrote to a thousand clubs in Lancashire offering a deal in which Dennis would play seven club members, giving them a total of 200 points start on a no-win, no-fee basis. The response from the clubs was tremendous and he was able to go to Australia with no financial worries. In Australia Dennis found himself playing his championship matches in different venues, with tiring journeys in between, but he reached the semi-final, losing to a fresher and more relaxed Eddie Charlton who had played all his matches in one place.

Dennis was now in great demand on the exhibition circuit and started to build up a lucrative career. In 1977 he again reached the semi-final of the World Championship, losing to Cliff Thorburn, and in 1979 he went all the way to the final but lost to Terry Griffiths in Terry's memorable year.

With all his club and tournament experience and his high status in the professional game, Dennis was still a desperately shy person. Whenever he was introduced to an audience he would blush furiously and with his red hair and high complexion he often looked like a little Belisha beacon holding a cue. In the beginning he had suffered agonies of embarrassment in speaking to a large audience and it was not until as recently as 1979–80 that his famous blush became much less frequent. Like many comedians and show people, Dennis turned to humour and developed an extrovert public personality to compensate for his natural diffidence and feelings of awkwardness. The public took to his friendly style and with a lot of work and study he grew into the part. For some years he has been one of the busiest professionals in the exhibition game and he relishes the clubs and respects their players perhaps more than any other professional player. He knows that the clubs made him what he is, provided him with a good living and turned him from a tongue-tied Irish lad into a mature and confident person. He likes himself better this way and has never forgotten his debt to the ordinary people in snooker.

In the tournaments the laughter has to stop and Dennis plays it straight and plays it well. Because of his image some players think that he is such a nice jolly fellow that he doesn't have to be taken seriously, but his record shows that he can beat the best in the world and play the toughest matches without wilting under pressure. He had the great satisfaction of taking the Irish Professional title from Alex Higgins in 1980 and successfully defended it against Patsy Fagan in 1981. He has yet to win a major British or world title, but if he shows his best form at the right time he must do so

When the laughing has to stop – Dennis concentrates hard during a tournament.

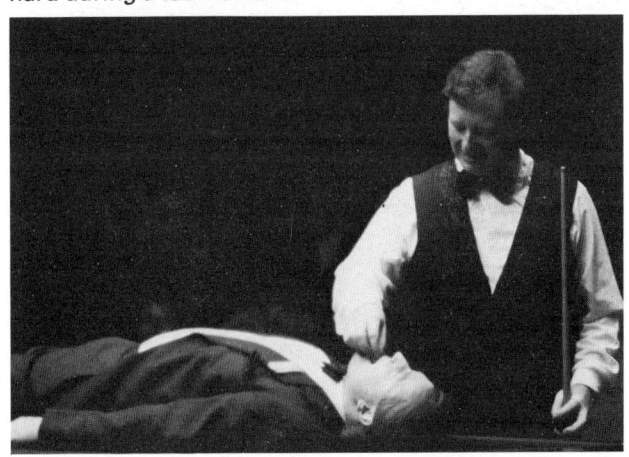

Taylor the entertainer – all that's needed for this shot is a brave volunteer, a cue ball and black, and Dennis's infallible Irish logic. The trick is to cue on the white, placed on the rail behind the victim, and hit the black without removing the victim's nose. And if the volunteer seems worried when all this is explained, Dennis reassures him, 'Wait till you see where I play the next shot from!' Photo: John Carty.

eventually. In the latter part of the seventies his inability to clinch a big title left a question mark on his record and some people thought that he was more of a nightclub comedian than serious contender. But his consistent record over the years has persuaded even the most cynical that Dennis has earned his place at the top. In the fiercely competitive conditions of modern snooker it simply isn't possible to maintain a high rating without talent and fighting spirit. Dennis has all of that.

It is far from easy to combine the demands of an entertaining club act with the pressures of tournament snooker but Dennis has done it, earning a high income and respect as a player. And as he leaves his audience laughing at the latest collection of Irish jokes, Dennis is laughing too – all the way to the bank.

12

Timing: the key to better snooker

Photo: Dave Muscroft.

I've been listening to arguments and taking part in them like all other snooker enthusiasts (I nearly said 'maniacs'!) for more years than I care to remember as to why one player plays better than another. Phrases, cliches, all the expressive terms describing stance, cue action, technique and so on are flogged to death. Not that I am complaining – long may it continue; the time to worry is when it stops. We all try to attach the success of any player to his sound technique or perhaps his cue action, yet if we could put a dozen famous names side by side it would be apparent that the differences in style, approach and cueing are vast. It is no wonder therefore that students of the game find it extremely hard to master, and punters argue all hours of the night, and just to keep the pot a-boiling I would like to throw in more food for thought.

The word 'timing' occurs far less than most other terms during discussions on technique and is used mostly as an expression of pleasure that a shot has been well played. 'He must work on his cue action' or 'He should check his stance' are frequent expressions, but how often do you hear 'He should practise his timing'? Not very often, if ever.

How can you account for Alex Higgins successfully smashing a ball into a pocket and ending up with his head under the shade and his cue tip almost stuck in the ear of someone in the front row, or Steve Davis playing a beautiful smooth cue action straight out of a coaching manual (I hope it's mine!) yet missing the black off its spot? Just for now, forget all the whys and wherefores and consider the facts. Alex has, according to the book, done it all wrong and got it right; Steve has done it right and got it wrong. My point is that timing in both cases is the cause of success and failure. Only the player involved senses the mistake he has made, whether he understands it or not, and shrugs it off as a bad shot for one reason or another. The problem is that timing is something which comes to you through a feeling of wellbeing and confidence in your own ability. It has to be of your own making, and it is the one aspect of the game that cannot be obtained from watching others, hence the mystery surrounding it. It is a most difficult subject to talk about in practical terms, yet a deeper working knowledge of what happens can often help to iron out weaknesses right through the whole approach to your every shot. This is my own personal theory which I have found, in my later years, to be invaluable in helping me to hold my form and even perhaps improve it.

Timing is co-ordination of all the body muscles working in conjunction governed by the brain. The messages registered with the brain, which are passed on to the body, come from the eye, so in that sense the brain is controlled by what the eye sees. From my own experience, the eyes search out the angles or lines of aim involved and during the

Opposite: Steve Davis. Photo: Dave Muscroft.

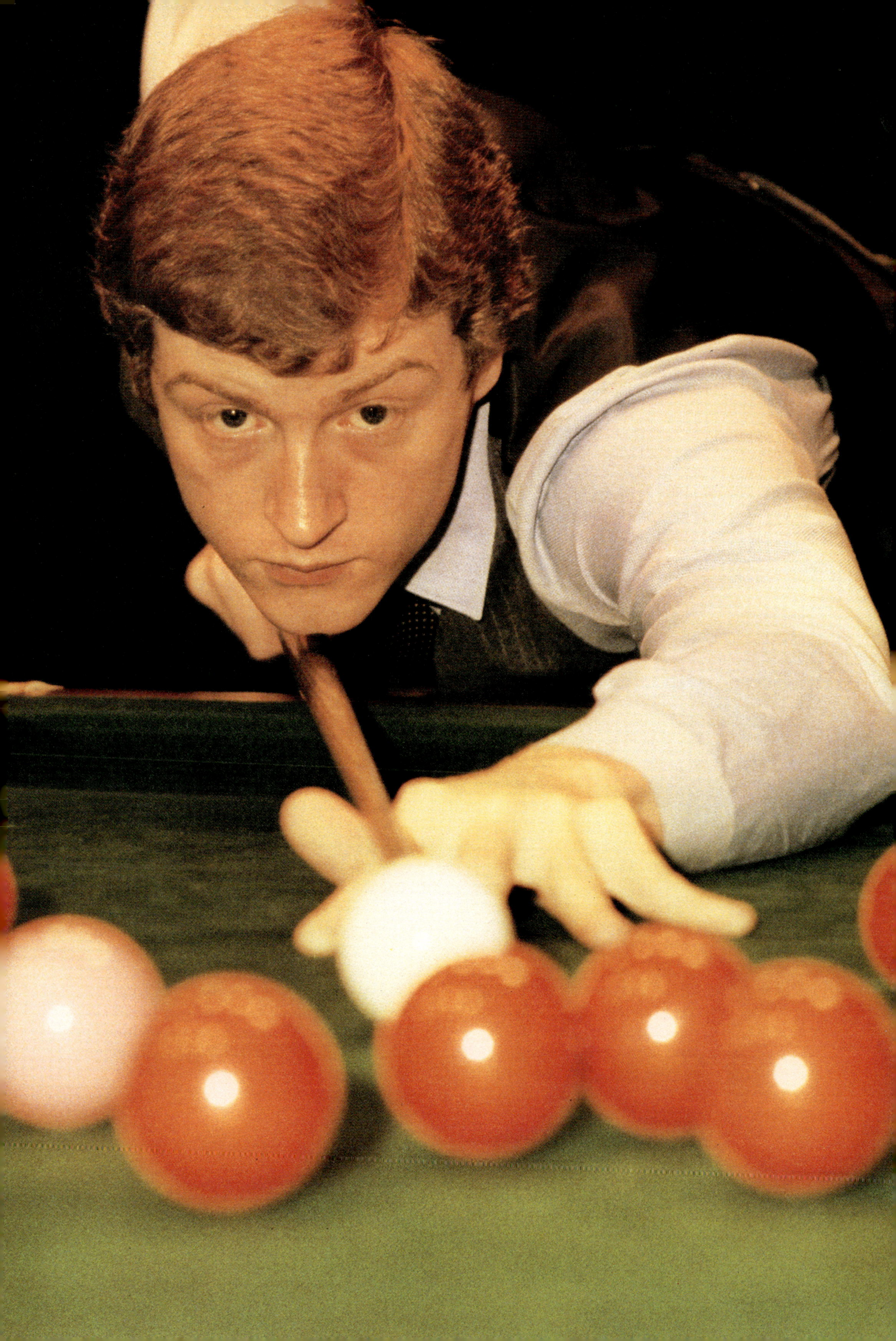

search there is an instant of complete recognition which should be distinguished from the searching period. That precise moment is the time when the tip should be following up to strike the cue ball, sending it on its way before the picture fades.

The more simple and easy the shot, the easier that fleeting glimpse of complete recognition is found and able to be prolonged, permitting an unhurried delivery. When a shot is really difficult, for whatever reason, the moment of recognition by the eyes cannot be held and prolonged so easily, which tends to encourage a snatchy or hurried action as you try to ensure contact at the correct time: this of course often produces the very action you are trying to avoid in your careful preamble to the shot. The whole purpose of preparation or preamble, which differs so much from player to player and can almost be called style, is to ensure that you play or deliver when you are given the message. So often the miss is not because you have misjudged the angle or lifted your head, but simply that the shot was mis-timed. The body reactions are a reflection of mis-timing, happening almost simultaneously because of it.

Let us say for discussion purposes that the perfect cue action is, at the moment of recognition of the shot, to be going forward in your last delivery striking the cue ball one-tenth of a second after recognition. If you are constantly missing, yet feel you have complete recognition, you are either striking two-tenths too soon or too late. This gives a feeling of having been in a void. At the moment of truth your eyes have gone back to searching instead of remaining on the job, so you haven't really seen the two balls meeting and going their separate ways. You may have anticipated the result and wandered to the expectant pocket or back to the cue ball. I am sure that the more advanced players searching for higher standards have experienced these feelings; whether they have interpreted them this way is another matter. The usual expression used to describe a failure of this kind is to say you 'moved on the shot'.

The way I have improved my own standard is by developing a mental attitude of anticipating the striking of the cue ball during my preamble, thus ensuring that my eyes are on the object ball momentarily longer, avoiding as much as possible

Alex Higgins. Photo: Dave Muscroft.

the task of bringing all my reactions to a peak at one fleeting moment. In the simplest terms, learn by practice to hold the moment of recognition slightly longer through good anticipation, thus giving yourself more time to play the stroke.

I would like to bet that if any of the professionals were asked, they would say that when they were down and lined up for a pot of reasonable proportions they never expect to miss as far as the physical aspect is concerned yet something happens within when they do, the root cause of which can be many things. This minor explosion between mental and physical aspects is brought about by hurried or hassled discomfort in bridging, playing over a ball, annoyance with the audience or when tucked up on the cushion. If you like, it is almost a moment of panic. It is the player who is able to combat this very natural human weakness, by imposing on himself a control of his physical and mental co-ordination through practice as I have tried to suggest, who will be more likely to succeed. The gifted players, who are few, can and do scoff at the breaking-down into method of how to play.

Once technique of stance and cue delivery have been reasonably mastered and a good understanding of the game has been achieved, it all becomes very much a case of state of mind. If you have all the ability in the world but no mind for the game, your ability is nothing, for all the world loves a winner.

13

I will survive

Snooker is a sport. It is also now a part of showbusiness. As in showbusiness, it generally takes ten years to produce an overnight star. In this chapter we look at four of the finest players in England, men who have seen the snooker world from both sides and believe, as we do, that despite the vagaries of fate there is a place in the sun for those on whom the gods have smiled.

David Taylor

In a qualifying round of the 1977 Embassy World Professional Championship David Taylor of Manchester played David Greaves of Blackpool at Fishers Snooker Centre, Acton, West London. The players were unlucky that this one match had been moved from the fairly luxurious setting of Hounslow Civic Chamber where all the other matches were being played, but the room at Fishers was a good matchroom with seating for 150 people. For this match there was an audience of three.

Taylor won, but as he drove away from Acton that night to find his way to Manchester he must have wondered, after eight years as a professional player, if he'd lost his way in snooker. The gap between himself and the players reaping the rewards of this blossoming game seemed as wide as the gap between the homely West London club and the glittering Crucible Theatre.

David had won the World Amateur Snooker Championship in 1968 and turned professional in 1969. It was acknowledged that he could play the game, that he was a friendly fellow, well liked by

David Taylor. Photo: Dave Muscroft.

other players. But his results in World Championships had been disastrous. He was always likely to come through qualifying rounds, to beat a few old-timers or new professionals, but as soon as he came up against seeded players he was destined to lose. He seemed to have all the shots, the talent and the knowledge to do much better but his 'Mr Nice Guy' image was carried too far into his snooker and no one could imagine David putting fear into the hearts of prospective opponents. He was a good lad, a nice player, a good work-out, but 'Who am I playing in the next round?' was the thought in the minds of many professionals when they saw that they were drawn against David Taylor. This attitude seemed to infect David too. He expected to do well, hoped to win, but did not show the confidence and aggression needed in the top flight of snooker. This was surprising because he *was* a world champion and no man can become champion of the world in any sport without it affecting his thinking for the rest of his life. No man can win the world amateur title without talent and a strong belief in himself. By 1977 the snooker world was beginning to wonder if David Taylor was proving these basic tenets to be untrue.

Curiously enough, he was making a good living at the game. Since 1971 he had had no other source of income but snooker and he was probably the only player at his level in the early seventies who did not have another job to support himself. He was contracted to the Pontins Holidays company, going round the various camps during the summer giving exhibitions, and this kept him solvent. 'I owe that to Ray Reardon,' David said. 'He was the Pontins professional and when he had to make a trip to South Africa in 1971 he put me forward as his replacement and Pontins signed me up. When he came back I expected to step down, but Ray spoke to Pontins and got them to leave me with my circuit of camps and he took a new circuit – keeping me in work and expanding the game a little bit at the same time!'

Although David had appeared in the television tournament 'Pot Black' in 1971, he had not appeared again and the invitations to any big tournaments were few or non-existent. He kept plugging away, entering everything he could, but with no great success – until 1978. In that year he reached the final of the Coral UK Championship, losing to Doug Mountjoy in the final. In the course of the championship he defeated the reigning champion Patsy Fagan, rising star John Virgo, and the biggest star of all, Alex Higgins. Before the championship started, Alex was a favourite in the betting while David was offered at 66-1. That championship was televized and David, with his good looks and striking silver hair, made a big impression with the public. Commentator Ted Lowe christened him 'the Silver Fox', he received a cheque for £2,000, the biggest prize of his career, and the players and the public looked at David Taylor with new eyes.

David had enjoyed this run of consistent good play and the thought was stirring in his mind that it would be nice to keep it going, or even improve it, in all championships. How was he to do it? Over a period of some months he and his wife Jan analysed

John Virgo. Photo: Dave Muscroft.

and discussed his game endlessly. New thinking was required and Jan provided it. 'Jan has been a very big influence on me,' David said. 'She's very knowledgeable about the game and she can go into all the technicalities with me. She's honest and objective and I found that very useful in getting my mind straight. I don't know how I would have made out if she knew nothing about the game or wasn't interested.'

With Jan's help David studied the methods of the most successful players and compared them with his own. Together they analysed photographs of each player and studied David's style to see where improvement could be made. 'But the biggest change had to be in my attitude,' David said. 'Jan showed me that. I needed to have a much more positive approach to the game, stop making excuses for defeat, work on my style. And that's what I did.'

The new regime worked. David's game improved and he was no longer an also-ran but a genuine contender to be treated with respect and caution. In 1980 he went all the way to the semi-final of the Embassy World Championship, beating Ray Edmonds, Fred Davis and Ray Reardon on the way. He lost in the semi-final to eventual champion, Cliff Thorburn, but he had, at last, arrived. The response from the public was staggering and it was clear that the television viewers had found a new pin-up boy. That was good for David, but from a professional player's point of view it was much more important to him that snooker had found a new top-class player. He was now one of the elite, and in 1981 his status was confirmed by his placing at number 7 in the world ratings, the highest position he had ever achieved. Again in 1981 he reached the final of a major tournament, the Yamaha International, losing to Steve Davis.

The real breakthrough was the 1980 World Championship rather than his earlier good showing in the UK, and since that time David has had all the work he wants. 'I won't do five or six exhibitions a week. I enjoy them, but I'm a family man and I don't want to be trailing all over the country every night. I'm not sure that exhibition snooker is good for my match play and I try to keep it down to two exhibitions a week. I'm happy with that,' he said.

The invitations to big tournaments, so important to a top professional, now pour in. David is back on 'Pot Black', that crucial showcase of snooker talent, and all is well in his world. Ability and talent still come first, but the story of David Taylor shows all too clearly that hard work must not be far behind. Here was a man gifted as few are gifted, who had reigned supreme as an amateur and struggled through the wastelands of professional snooker, a man who had won, had lost, had been lost and yet had found the way in the most competitive age the game has known.

The new, positive David Taylor relishes it all: 'I enjoy everything about the game,' he said. 'The worst thing about it – about any professional sport – is playing badly and being frustrated. Of course the competition is tougher today. In the early seventies John Spencer and Ray Reardon were in a class of their own. Nowadays there are ten or twelve players of about that standard. Look at Jimmy White – he's tremendous. He loses stupid matches, he always will, but he's bound to win most of the big ones too. The increased pressure in matches I can stand. When you're playing well it's a bed of roses, and I'd much rather be in at the top, playing the best players in the world when I'm playing well, than struggling to find my form in the lower ranks.'

Twelve years of trying have left him with a philosophy: 'In the end you've got to do it with your cue,' he says. 'All the talk, the advertising, everything else is irrelevant. I think that some of the new players coming into the professional game think that the world or the WPBSA owes them something. It doesn't. I've seen it from both sides and however much of a cliché it may be, the truth is that you only succeed by results.' David's experience might demonstrate to impatient young professionals that success perhaps also requires one or both of those rare and precious commodities, time – and the love of a good woman.

John Virgo

John Virgo was in danger of becoming famous as the man who never smiled on television. He had been one of the outstanding amateurs of his day and when he turned professional in 1977 his forthright manner and questioning attitude was like a bucket of cold water thrown over the cosy arrangements of professional snooker. The game mattered to John Virgo and if he made enemies in saying his piece, that was unlucky for them. It was also, of course, unlucky for him, as few of the established professionals would go out of their way to offer him cancelled bookings or opportunities of that sort. He had to fend for himself.

He wanted to be a winner. As an amateur he had given his opinions of most players and there was a pressure on him to show that he was as good as his publicity said. There was also the pressure of having to make a living at the game. John turned professional just before the really big tournaments became so common and he knew that while the tournaments would make his name, the club exhibition circuit would make his income. His morose appearance on television is not a true indication of his character but is merely the way that high concentration affects him. When he is not at the table he is a gregarious and talkative man who likes a good laugh. It was this side of his character that was to be his salvation, because he developed an act for his exhibition appearances that has earned him the title 'Snooker's Number One Entertainer' and kept him very busy. While other players do trick shots and jokes, John does trick shots and piercingly accurate impressions of his fellow professionals. He is a gifted mimic and can immediately conjure up Alex Higgins, Ray Reardon, Terry Griffiths and all the rest.

John is a great fan of Jackie Rea and has long been of the opinion that Jackie did more than anyone to keep the game alive in the old days, even if he had to become a comedian to do it. 'He's snooker's outstanding candidate for an OBE for services to the game,' says John emphatically. Coming from Manchester, John had always mixed with Spencer and Higgins and he used to impersonate them to amuse his friends. He watched Jackie Rea's act because it was the most successful at the time. 'Jackie used to do a few impressions,' John said. 'They were terrible – but people laughed. I worked on mine and one night, after a four-man exhibition show, I was called from the bar to do some trick shots. The tricks weren't working very well so I said, "I'm going to do something different", and I did the impersonations. They went down very well and surprised everyone – especially me – I never thought I'd have the courage to do them!'

When the word went round that John had a very entertaining act the bookings started to come in and this helped to relieve the tremendous pressure he was under as a tournament player. First, there was his big reputation and only two or three tournaments a year in which to prove himself; second, the financial pressure was always at the forefront of his mind and he could not play his best snooker. 'It's a bit difficult to relax and concentrate when you're trying to get through to the next round just to pay the electricity bill,' John said. His financial worries ended in 1978. He had just been beaten by David Taylor in the Coral UK Championship and was so disgusted with his form that he considered giving up the game. His girl friend Avril, always a motive force behind him, persuaded him to talk to London manager, Henry West. 'That was the best thing that happened to me,' John said, 'Henry took me over. His other player, Patsy Fagan, was doing the Warners Holiday circuit and didn't want to continue with it. I became Warners professional and this, together with my bookings, meant that my income was

John Virgo. Photo: Dave Muscroft.

secure. I could concentrate on playing.'

John concentrated so well that he won the Coral UK Championship in 1979 and followed this up by winning the Bombay International against a top-quality field. With these results and a reputation on the club circuit, he became one of the game's highest earners. But whether he's winning or losing, the act is what everyone wants to see. In the early days he was doing a show with Ray Reardon, and out of deference to Ray he omitted the Reardon impression. 'What about me?' Ray asked, 'I thought you did me.' So John 'did' Ray, perhaps the cruellest of his impressions, and Ray laughed with everyone else. 'I get a lot of complaints, especially about the Reardon impression,' says John. 'I tell a few jokes about him, and in the last year or so when he hasn't been doing very well some spectators have said that's unfair. It's not meant to be, I have a great respect for Ray but he has so many mannerisms he's a godsend to me. Higgins and Spencer were my star pieces, but when Spencer went out of the picture for a few years I couldn't get any response when I did him. The audiences in clubs only recognize players who've been on television and John hadn't had much exposure in his lean period – a lot of the audience didn't know who he was.'

John's impressions are so good that they cause everyone to look at the subject in a new light: did Terry Griffiths really take so long to play a shot, flick his hair and sway about before John started doing him, or has he been watching John Virgo? 'Everyone has their little habits,' John said. 'I'm still working on my Steve Davis and I've only just noticed another thing he does. I think my Cliff Thorburn is my best impression, but unfortunately the audiences just don't find it funny. Usually I do Terry Griffiths, who's slow like Cliff, then I say, "Well, I can't do Cliff Thorburn now or we'll be here all night." Any player can be impersonated, although I may have trouble with some of the younger ones who are left-handed. It comes quite naturally to me. I've listened to professional impressionists talking and I have the same feeling they have – as soon as I stick my backside out and sniff I *am* John Spencer!'

John has now recruited a professional scriptwriter to keep his act fresh – the first player to do so – and he'll obviously remain in great demand on the exhibition circuit. 'I should do,' John said; 'some players' fees have risen to astronomical levels. They forget there's a recession on. I'm one of the few players the ordinary clubs can afford!'

John was disappointed with his tournament record in 1981. 'Maybe I wasn't hungry enough after winning the UK title,' he said, 'but I haven't lost my love for the game. That's the most important thing in trying to stay at the top. I practise regularly for six or seven hours a day. To my mind, six hours of hard practice is about equal to six frames in a tournament. It's no use saying six frames only take two hours, therefore you'll only practise for two hours – you've got to equal the effort, not the time.'

John lived up to that opinion one night at Kingston Snooker Centre. Together with Cliff Thorburn and Kirk Stevens he played 'points' snooker for practice and the session lasted seventeen and a half hours! 'But at the end I was playing as well as I've ever done. It becomes so natural you don't have to think about it,' said John. He is convinced that some of the older stars don't practise enough. 'Two weeks before the Embassy World Championship isn't enough. That's why some of the younger players have such an advantage – they're never away from a table.' John is keeping to the same good habit and making sure that, despite his busy life, he will be a professional champion again. 'I want to be known as snooker's number one player, not snooker's number one entertainer,' he said, doing an incredibly accurate impression of John Virgo.

Willie Thorne

The great and enduring mystery of professional snooker is this: why isn't Willie Thorne a champion? The twenty-eight-year-old from Leicester was British Boys' Champion in billiards and snooker in 1970, British Junior Billiards Champion from 1970 to 1973 and British Junior Snooker Champion in 1973. He was Southern Area Champion in 1975 and lost in the final of the English Championship of that year to Sid Hood of Grimsby. He turned professional in 1977, having been invited to play on television's 'Pot Black' although he was an amateur. Before he could set the precedent of an amateur appearing on 'Pot Black' he was swiftly granted professional status.

Willie Thorne is one of the most natural players in the game, with a smooth flowing action that has led him to compile nearly a thousand century breaks. His tactical appreciation is sound but he loses important matches when he is in with a good chance because he tends to rely on his great skills always being at a peak – which is not the way the game works. Willie will make a nice break of fifty or sixty and have his adversary in deep trouble, yet go for just one ball too many. In more relaxed games he would pot that ball but in the big matches discretion is often the better part of valour and the bold shot can betray the attacking player. It is not in Willie's nature to be a plodder and he cannot resist backing his judgment that the shot *will* go. It only needs to fail once or twice in a 17-frame match to leave Willie out of the running for another year. His record is one of close defeats, usually in excellent matches. No one goes to sleep when Willie is around, but whether the score is 9-8 or 9-0 the loser is still left pondering what went wrong while his opponent goes on to greater things.

Willie is one of the most popular men in snooker and greatly in demand on the exhibition circuit both at home and abroad. If Rupert Brooke was the handsomest man in England it may be said that the younger Willie Thorne was the handsomest man in snooker! In that department he now has competition from the young newcomers, but he still doesn't look too bad! He is urbane, witty, a non-drinker but a speed-mad driver, an easy talker and he makes a good impression wherever he goes. Some commentators, trying to find the answer to the enigma of Willie Thorne, feel that perhaps he's just too nice, or, as one reporter callously observed, 'He's got to learn to enjoy putting the boot in in his matches.'

Willie did not have a good competitive start in 1981 and it was made worse when he broke both legs in a go-karting accident. Less than three weeks

Willie Thorne. Photo: Dave Muscroft.

after the accident he was planning to compete in the Jameson International Open, with plaster on both legs and a friend standing behind him in case he fell over! But the effort was too much, too soon, and Willie had to withdraw. A month later, with one of his feet still in plaster, he played through his early rounds of the Coral UK Championship and successfully qualified. Also while still in plaster he achieved a rare and surely inviolate record when he became the first man to make a maximum break in plaster! He achieved this feat at his snooker centre in Leicester and it was his fourteenth maximum break. It pleased his fans and it pleased Willie. But nothing would please him and his many friends more than a good win in a tournament to do justice to his undoubted skills.

Patsy Fagan

Patsy Fagan, the Dubliner who has been adopted by London since he settled there eight years ago, found that the glare of the spotlight can be as cruel and uncompromising as it is flattering and rewarding. He was one of the men most likely to succeed when he turned professional in 1977. He had been a great favourite as an amateur all over the country and although his cue action was not technically perfect, his grip being rather too light, he was expected to establish himself in the front ranks of professional snooker.

He was always a bit shy and did not find it easy to express himself, but on the table the cue said it all for him. He was a match player first and foremost; not a trick-shot specialist, not a comedian. What he liked best and did best was beating people, especially if there were thousands of pounds at stake. He and those around him knew that as a professional he would have to live by tournament results. In his first year he did that very well, winning the United Kingdom Championship (then sponsored by the Composition Ball Company) and a month later claiming victory in the Dry Blackthorn Tournament with a first prize of £2,000 against Ray Reardon and Alex Higgins.

Patsy had a steady season in 1978, including a high-pressure win over Alex Higgins in the Embassy World Championship, and was rated eleventh in the world that year. From about the middle of 1979, however, he developed a psychological 'block' when using the rest. At first it seemed to be just a touch of clumsiness but soon, whenever he played with the rest, he was unable to let the cue go through to complete the shot. He could not release it but continued with the normal back-and-forth movement for an interminable time, eventually lungeing at the ball and miscueing. He had been one of the world's best players with the rest and no explanation could be found for this strange affliction. It soon demoralized him and affected the rest of his game. 'I was playing left-handed, playing to avoid ever having to use the rest while my opponents soon realized that a good safety shot against me was any shot where I had to use the rest,' said Patsy. This type of problem is known in golf, particularly in putting, and is often called 'the yips', but nothing quite like it had been seen in snooker. His then manager, Henry West, together with Patsy's father-in-law, Derek Saunders, and his family, tried to get him to psychiatrists, doctors, hypnotists, but to no avail. It reached the stage where good friends and supporters of Patsy would not book him for an exhibition in case they caused him embarrassment if he 'froze' on their show. In televized matches Patsy's problem was exposed to the world, adding further to the burdens upon him. He practised for hours with the rest, played well in practice, seemed to have overcome the problem, but it would return: 'It's like watching a boy scout trying to start a fire,' said one observer.

Patsy faced the problem and worked on it. He did not withdraw from any tournaments but, puzzled and hurt by his curse, hoped time would cure it. 'He never dodged the issue,' said Derek Saunders. 'We would sit and discuss it for hours, days, trying to find the reason. I even suggested once that deep inside he didn't want to play, didn't want to win or be famous – that he was giving himself an excuse to seek obscurity. He considered that idea carefully, but didn't agree.'

Time did heal the aberration. Constant practice with his friends at the Ron Gross Centre and the support and love of his wife Elaine and her close-knit family led him to longer and longer periods without problems. The century breaks were going in again, he was playing with the rest as well

Photo: Dave Muscroft.

as he ever had, enjoying his snooker and keen to get to the table once more.

In March 1981 he met Dennis Taylor for the All-Ireland Professional title in Coleraine. Patsy played like his old self, all doubt and uncertainty removed. He won the first four sessions to lead by 19 frames to 15. Dennis came back, playing some of his best snooker to win 5 frames in a row, but still Patsy pushed him to 21-21, only to lose on the last frame. It could so easily have gone his way, but the important thing was that Fagan was back on form and the Coleraine crowd rose to him as well as to the champion. Later in the year he was the backbone of the Republic of Ireland team in the State Express World Team Classic, ensuring that Ireland qualified at the expense of Scotland and scoring wins over Ray Reardon and Kirk Stevens in the competition proper.

It's still a long way back for Patsy Fagan, but if he can relax in the knowledge that his dreadful problem has gone he will fulfil all the great promise of a few years ago. In August of 1981 he and Elaine had their first child, a boy named Liam. Patsy, the proud father, never one for boasting, is now also the proud player, 'I'll do it for my little boy. I'll be a champion again,' he says.

14
Women's world of snooker

Even in the sweatiest male sports women have had a part to play. In the rugby or cricket club they are usually somewhere in the background making the sandwiches and offering bandages and sympathy to the wounded. There is no tradition of 'the little woman' in snooker. In the past many men quite literally 'escaped' to the social club or billiard hall in the sure and happy knowledge that the steward or manager would never let a woman set foot in there. There was no place for women either on the table or behind the scenes, and the only time they played any noticeable part in the man's game was when it provided a living for the family – when the husband was a professional player making reasonable money from the game. A few mothers encouraged and supported their sons, but wives and girlfriends generally regarded the game as a rival for their man's attentions. To add insult to injury, they often had to listen to a ball-by-ball replay of his best or worst matches. After twenty years of marriage a wife can listen to this sort of commentary with the same enthusiasm and understanding that she would give to a recital of the Moscow telephone directory. In extreme cases patience wore through to undisguised loathing and resentment for the game: many a promising relationship has foundered on man's obsession with knocking a lot of little coloured balls around with a big stick.

In the dark ages of snooker (say, during the fifties and sixties) women did not or would not and in many cases could not watch 'live' snooker. If they never watched it they could hardly become attracted to it, and it is not surprising that women players were a very rare breed. But they did exist. From the time of Mary Queen of Scots (who enjoyed billiards) women did play, but only in private houses and it tended to be the case that only the upper classes played – a reflection of the aristocratic origins of billiards and snooker but also a force of circumstance, because without a table in the home a woman could not find anywhere to play. From the 1930s onwards there were women's official championships and a handful gained real proficiency at the games. While it would be ungallant to say that the typical player of that age looked as if she had grown up with a hockey stick in her hand, there was, nevertheless, the impression that they had jolly well decided what sport they were taking up and no mere man would stop them. They had a hearty independence which suggested that the moment they put down their cue they'd be able to drive an ambulance through a blitz or know six ways to start a fire without matches.

Something of a new era in women's snooker began in 1954 when the seventeen-year-old Maureen Barrett won the English title. She went on to win that title a record eight times (after her marriage, as Maureen Baynton) and won the women's billiards title five times. 'I was about the first ordinary working-class girl in the game,' Maureen recalls. 'The other players were either upper class or upper middle class when I started, but they were all quite pleasant to me.'

Maureen had started to play snooker at the age of ten when recuperating from rheumatic fever, having first seen a table at Peckham Health Centre, a forerunner of the modern leisure centre. 'I needed fairly gentle exercise and I thought that snooker might be the game for me. I had plenty of help from other players at the centre and they taught me the basics,' Maureen said. 'I picked it up quite easily and although I wasn't a child prodigy, I was proficient enough to attract the attention of the top female professional, Joyce Gardner, and the BBC. We did a series of radio programmes in the early fifties in which Joyce would describe what I was doing and explain what I should be doing. We spent the whole of one programme discussing the selection of my first good cue.'

When Maureen was twelve the Peckham Health Centre closed down and she started to play at Lewisham Temperance Hall. 'It was difficult to find a place to play, partly because of my age, but mainly because I was female. I could never, in those days, just walk into a billiard hall. I'd need to know in advance that it was all right and that they'd accept me. Some of the billiard halls in London were no place for a young lady! I always had trouble getting a game. When I was about sixteen I went to Butlin's Holiday Camp in Brighton where they had about twenty-three tables, but they wouldn't let me play – no women allowed, even if I was the British schoolgirl champion!'

WOMEN'S WORLD OF SNOOKER

Maureen Baynton. Photo: John Carty.

In Maureen's early days the women's championship was played at Burroughes and Watts Hall, but when this closed down in 1966 the ladies moved to Herbert Holt's club in Windmill Street, Soho. It did not have the atmosphere of the hallowed Burroughes and Watts match room, but the girls were glad of any venue for their official matches.

By about 1968 Maureen felt that there was little point in remaining in the amateur game. She decided to turn professional. Before the war there had been a group of women professionals but by 1968 only Joyce Gardner was still active. 'Turning professional' was a rather obscure action: what she did was to declare herself a professional, unavailable for any amateur championships. It was a grey area, but in Maureen's case the result was immediate – 'It meant I retired,' said Maureen. 'There was nothing doing for a woman professional.'

In the sixties the women's game, like the professional game, was in the doldrums and Maureen had 'retired' to concentrate on family life and raising daughter Wendy (herself now a promising junior player). There didn't seem to be much left to achieve.

'I suppose that the biggest change between 1954 and 1968 was that the old-style women players had disappeared and been replaced by ordinary women. The sort of women who were chauffeur-driven to matches were no longer around,' Maureen said, 'but I suppose that was a social trend even outside of snooker. The new girls in the game were still fairly independent – single girls who took the trouble to become involved in it. Sometimes, if they were quite young, their parents would support them, but usually they were on their own. I think the biggest difference in the last seven years since I returned to the game is that husbands and boyfriends now come along and actively support their women, often giving up their own game to ensure that their wife or girlfriend has every chance. That's very much a new thing.'

What brought Maureen back into the game was a tournament that set a spark to women's snooker and quite clearly stands as the growth point of the modern game. In 1976 Embassy was persuaded to sponsor the World Professional Snooker Championship for the first time and, luckily for the women, the promotor of that championship, Maurice Hayes, arranged an amateur tournament and a women's tournament as supporting features. So the word went out that a women's tournament, offering a first prize of £500 and an expensive watch, would be held in Middlesbrough. 'I saw people there that I hadn't seen for ten years,' Maureen recollects. 'Some of them hadn't played since just after the war but they turned out in force for this competition.' (Maureen was beaten in the semi-final by Muriel Hazeldine who had won the women's title twice since Maureen's retirement, and in the final Vera Selby, the Newcastle art lecturer who had dominated the game since Maureen's departure, beat Muriel). The tournament had reminded all the girls that they were still around. The newspapers showed considerable interest in their efforts and they all had the feeling that something good would now happen in the women's game.

Nothing did. But 1977 was the year of the Queen's Silver Jubilee, an excuse for tournaments of all sorts. The women players received an invitation from Walter West, a noted London amateur player and then manager of the Pot Black Club, Clapham, to compete in a ladies' competition. West was a player of real ability with an incredible number of century breaks to his credit. He was also a man of some foresight and he could see that the coming rise of the boy wonders in snooker would make it difficult for him to add to the British Junior title he had won in 1957. Yet he was a man determined to carve out his own place in snooker and it was the good fortune of the women that he spotted the potential in their game.

Following the success of the Jubilee tournament, West staged a further event at the Wandsworth Billiards Club. Interest was now at a high level and women who had never before entered serious

Walter West, who has worked so hard for women's snooker. Photo: John Carty.

competitions joined in to play some of the country's leading ladies. More than 250 spectators watched the final stages of this event. West offered to organize women's snooker, but only if he were voted in as chairman and secretary of their official governing body, and this was duly done. 'He did a lot for women's snooker,' Maureen says. 'He was a good player himself and I think he was frustrated at his own lack of success as a player. He put a lot of energy into organizing the game and obtaining sponsors. One of the first things he did was to arrange a women's international match between England and Ireland – a fantastic idea.' That match was played at the Fairview Club, Dublin, sponsored by leading Irish snooker figure Terry Rogers. England won the match and the ladies were royally treated in Dublin, but there were certain gaps in the administrative arrangements and much recrimination between Messrs Rogers and West. The return match was never played.

Walter West was adamant that his association was a world organization and not merely a vehicle for English women. He spent untold hours on the telephone making contact with players in New Zealand, Australia and Canada, and perhaps the greatest achievement of his reign was to bring these women together in a full appreciation of each other's existence. He did more: through his talent for finding sponsors and raising money he actually brought them together to compete against each other in England – something that would have seemed impossible a few years earlier.

In 1980 West, with the sponsorship of Guinness, staged the first Women's World Championship at Warner's Holiday Village, Hayling Island. Once again this was a supporting event to a 'main' tournament that featured many of the leading male professionals and amateurs. Much to the chagrin of the (different) sponsors of the main tournament, and to the delight of Walter and the girls, their championship 'stole' the publicity and achieved more coverage than the major tournament. The reasons for all the publicity were confused: many reporters from national newspapers came along expecting to see luscious blondes cavorting around the table in bikinis; others just saw a human interest story in the fact that women could so invade a man's world; the cynical were spurred by Doctor Johnson's dictum regarding female preachers, 'It is rather like seeing a dog dancing on its hind legs. It is not that it is done well, but one is surprised to see it done at all.' In fact it was done very well, and this championship thrust into the spotlight some of the players who are clearly going to figure prominently

Lesley McIlraith of Australia. Photo: John Carty.

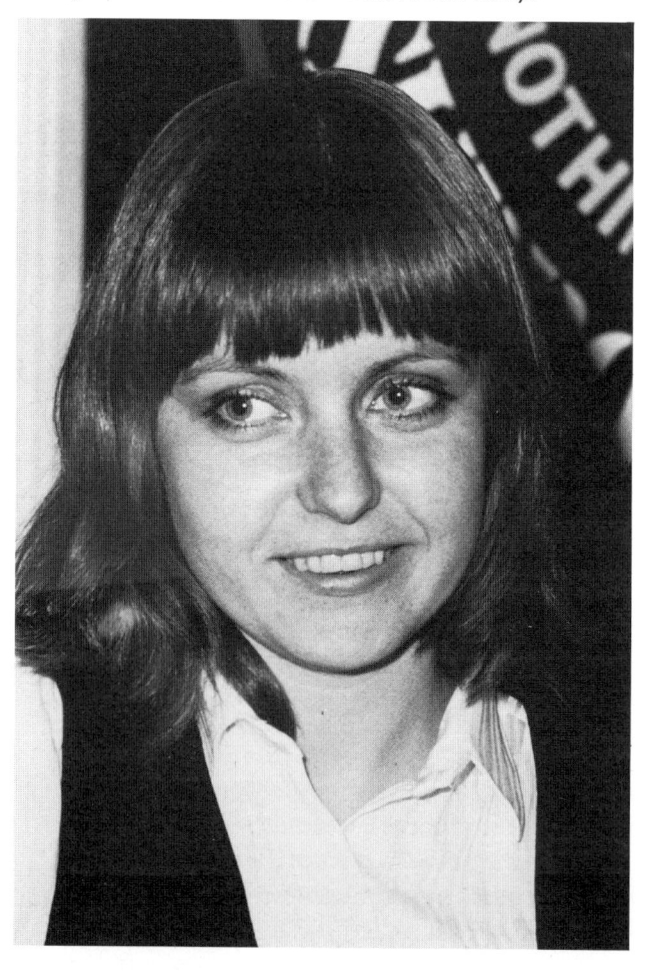

WOMEN'S WORLD OF SNOOKER

in any development of women's snooker.

The Australian Lesley McIlraith won the championship, beating Agnes Davies of Wales 4-2 in the final, and it seemed that, despite the higher level of activity in Britain, the home-based girls would have their work cut out to match the standard set by Lesley.

The Canadians turned up in force for the match: Natalie Stelmach, the only woman then to have made a century break, three-times winner of the CNE ladies' title, a fine player with all-round skills and a very likely candidate for a future world title; Sue LeMaich of Hamilton, Ontario, a very steady player who shows great composure and potting ability; the determined and career-minded fine-art graduate, Mary-Ann McConnell; the vivacious Japanese-Canadian, Grace Cayley. Many people searching for a woman player with star quality will look beyond potting ability to attributes such as prettiness and charm. Unfair to women? Of course, but so are many things in this life. While Grace Cayley has yet to reach the standard of play of the very best women, she has that great asset, personality. Her game will improve because she is on the right lines in playing an attractive, attacking game, and if women are to feature on television – and they will – Grace must be picked as a possible star of the future.

Grace Cayley. Photo: Dave Muscroft.

Top Canadian players (from left) Natalie Stelmach, Grace Cayley and Sue LeMaich. Photo: John Carty.

Somewhere among the UK-based players is probably the woman who will become the first superstar of female snooker, if only because the opportunities seem more promising in the UK.

Vera Selby of Newcastle lost in the quarter-finals of the 1980 championship, but went on to become world champion in 1981. She is a gracious and talented player, but her style is very much of the old regime: safety first, stop your opponent potting a ball, then take what little is going. Vera's exemplary record shows that so far these tactics have worked, but they are twenty years out of date and cannot survive the onslaught of the aggressive newcomers.

Ann Johnson of Cheltenham, twice winner of the

Vera Selby, Women's World Champion 1981.

Photo: John Carty.

Ann Johnson. Photo: John Carty.

English title, has obvious potential. Like Vera Selby, she performs creditably in a snooker league each week and has shown real dedication in ensuring that she can play the game regularly and play it well. An attractive and consistent player, she has yet to win full reward for her skills.

Making her first appearance in the 1980 championship was a girl who went on to become an unlucky losing finalist in 1981, a young woman for whom a glittering future is confidently predicted. Her name is Mandy Fisher. She has style, she has skill, she has potential. In what may be the greatest possible insult to a lady player, it must be said: she plays like a man.

Mandy started by playing pool, but she was introduced to her Cambridgeshire neighbour, Fred Peck, in 1978. Fred is a well-known snooker buff and a local promotor of professional snooker. On his table at his home he gave Mandy a few lessons, declared that she had the makings of a fine player, and introduced her to the official women's game. She entered the English Ladies' Championship, which was staged in 1979 at the Cranewater Club, Southsea. At that time, having played for less than a year, her highest break was a very creditable 37. 'I was stuck on that for a year,' said Mandy. 'When I first started to play at Fred Peck's I knew nothing about any organized snooker. I didn't even know who Alex Higgins was. It was just me and the balls and the table. I found it totally fascinating, but it was just the personal challenge of it, trying to see what I could do.'

When she went to the Craneswater Club Mandy was impressed with the standard of play of Ann Johnson and Sian Newbury. 'By that time I knew that the standard of women's snooker wasn't the same as men's, but it still seemed too good for me. Little Sian was slamming in balls the length of the table and I didn't think I could ever play like her,' said Mandy.

On her return home, Mandy's enthusiasm

Mandy Fisher. Photo: John Carty.

infected her parents and they sacrificed their sitting-room to provide her with her own table as a Christmas present. It made a big difference to her progress because she no longer had any problems in finding somewhere to practise. It was undoubtedly a financial as well as a family sacrifice but, says Mandy gratefully, 'My mum and dad thought I would have a future in the game.' She left school at sixteen and for a while had a job as a sales clerk. A telephone call from Walter West, telling her of the 1981 World Championship to be sponsored by Guinness with a £2,000 first prize, prompted her decision to give up work and become a full-time player. 'I knew it was something worth practising for. I had been knocked out of the 1980 World Championship by Fran Lovis of Australia and I was determined to do better this time.' So Mandy left work and began to practise eight hours a day. Although she is cautious about taking exhibition bookings (fearing that too much will be expected or that the exhibition circuit does not provide the best experience), she has had some bookings and charges a fee of £75 for an evening.

When Mandy gave up her job, money was the most pressing problem. She took a Sunday market stall in her home town of March and filled it with all the bits and pieces from home that were not wanted. Having sold all of this, she was able to re-stock from a warehouse and provide herself with an enterprising living. However, Mandy gave up the stall to concentrate on snooker. She plays an average of twenty hours each week and has been rewarded with a highest break of 96 (6 blacks, 4 pinks and the colours up to pink). Prior to that, her highest break had been 60 exactly but, as so often happens, instead of progressing steadily through 60s and 70s she surprised herself with the 96. She has a boyfriend 'on and off' who rejoices in the name of Muscles. He too plays snooker, but his game has been cast into the shadows by Mandy's progress. 'Snooker is too important to me,' she says, 'I'm too young to be serious and Muscles knows that and supports me.' A very sensible lad, is Muscles, because if anyone were looking for the female equivalent of Steve Davis in a few years time they would go no further than the attractive Mandy Fisher of March.

And if we're right – if Mandy Fisher is the potential Steve Davis of women's snooker – where is their Jimmy White? She is alive and well, playing darts in Neath, West Wales. As we all now know, Jimmy White burst on the scene potting more balls than any youngster, showing a flair that surpassed almost anything that had gone before. The ladies' game has just such a player in the bashful nineteen-year-old Sian Newbury.

Sian Newbury. Photo: John Carty.

Sian, from a famous snooker family with dad a former international and brother Steve the best amateur in Wales, has not lived up to all the predictions made for her by the experts three years ago. She was then spoken of as potentially the best woman player there has been. She had the dramatic flair to pot balls from any angle, a reliable cue action that put her streets ahead of any sixteen-year-old in the world. But somehow she lost her way.

Sian never had any choice about taking up snooker: 'I had to play snooker,' she says with a smile. 'Both my dad and my brother played and my mum works in the snooker club. I couldn't do anything else.' She has played serious snooker since she was ten years old and although it wasn't entirely her own idea to take up the game, she claims to be self-taught. 'I had some help from dad and Steve, and especially from Mario Berni, but really I did it myself,' Sian said.

In recent years she has been feeling the pressures

of a snooker family and a snooker public, their expectations weighing upon her, and she has reacted by joining a darts league. She works as a sales assistant in the local Co-op, and although the owner of the Mackworth Club in Neath gives her free table time she is not always certain to get a game. 'I go down there intending to have two or three hours' play and some nights I can't even get a table. Of course it's frustrating, but I can't have everything my own way. It would be too much to expect the club to reserve a table for me to play for nothing when there are paying customers waiting,' Sian said. The weekends are not much help because Sian works on Saturdays – 'and I can't get up on Sunday mornings!' Her father, David, is naturally concerned about her lack of progress and application. 'He's always nagging me about it,' says Sian.

In any pro-am mixed doubles Sian is always partnered by Terry Griffiths and he has offered to coach her at his table at home in Llanelli. In amateur doubles she is partnered by brother Steve. 'When we play as pairs we never tell each other what to do. He always says, "If you want to know something, just ask" – but I never ask. In 1980 we won a big pairs tournament at Kingston in Surrey, but John Virgo got all the publicity as runner-up because he had only found his partner a couple of weeks before. Sometimes you can't win!'

Sian plays squash and darts of a fairly high standard: 'It's not the same as snooker – not the skill in it, is there? If snooker really takes off for women I might give up my job and practise full time.' She has played World Champion Vera Selby six times and always beaten her. A few years ago she made a television documentary with veteran Agnes Davies, also of Wales, and Sian made breaks of 39 and 20 on television. 'The programme was recorded and they tricked it up to make it look as if it was Agnes making those breaks. We were both upset about it, but what can you do?' Sian had played Ann Johnson about ten times and had always lost to her. Following a match in 1980, Sian turned to Ann and said, 'You're never going to beat me again.' And she never has. Sian doesn't know what made her say it or where the sudden resolve came from – but she needs more of that positive attitude if she is to take her place among the ranks of snooker's first ladies.

There is as much variety among the women players today as there is among the men. Young, old, married, single, steady tacticians, crazy potters, temperamental prima donnas and stolid journeymen. They have at last captured the imagination of the promoters and the public and we will surely see them competing on television in the

Agnes Davies. Photo: John Carty.

near future. The most likely development initially is a pro-am mixed doubles. Part of the 1981 Guinness World Championship package on the Isle of Wight was a mixed pairs championship. This turned out to be a very interesting tournament with the women players ably complementing the superior skills of their top professional partners. The title was won by Cliff Thorburn and Natalie Stelmach, but many of the women players made a good impression, adapting their natural game to suit the requirements of their partners. The key to the Thorburn/Stelmach success was the way in which Natalie curtailed her normal attacking style and played a safety game. She potted any loose balls on offer but otherwise did not lead her partner into any trouble with over-ambitious shots. Grace Cayley gave a good account of herself partnering Tony Meo, while Vera Selby, with the women's crown freshly in her grasp, was a sound partner for John Virgo – a pairing which was rather unlucky to lose in the absorbing final.

Apart from organized tournaments, the 'mixed doubles' idea is catching on in the exhibition circuit and some of the top women are starting to see a lucrative career in this field. Sue Foster of Tamworth in Staffordshire, a semi-finalist in the 1981 World Championship and a quarter-finalist in

WOMEN'S WORLD OF SNOOKER

Sue Foster. Photo: John Carty.

1980, has been invited by Terry Griffiths to appear in some of his exhibition engagements and she has done short tours with him, receiving a fee of £50 and expenses per evening.

Sue is a housewife with an eight-year-old son, but she finds time to practise for about three hours a day. Her husband Martin has more or less given up his own snooker to help Sue's career along. She has a highest break of 60 and, like Mandy Fisher, reckons to have earned over £1,000 in prizes and fees in each of the last few years. Also like Mandy, Sue turns out for matches in a very fetching professional outfit – a feminine version of the boring old male evening dress, but on these girls it looks different. 'We wanted to present a smart and up-to-date image,' Sue said, 'so Mandy and I decided we'd buy this style of trouser suit. It's comfortable to play in and it saves us clashing with our clothes when we meet in matches. We thought it would look professional and attractive, and judging by the comments we get I think we were right.'

How good are the women players? Well, it's relative. Compared to Alex Higgins, they're not very good; compared to the ordinary joe on table 9 in the billiard hall, they're brilliant. The best of the women are now probably of a standard equal to that of a reasonably good league player – and that is not a bad standard. They have improved beyond all recognition in the last three or four years. They have begun to adopt a more aggressive style and as a result we are starting to see breaks of 30, 40 or 50-odd, in the tense conditions of championship matches. In the 1981 Canadian Championship final Natalie Stelmach made a break of 56 – a record – in beating Mary Ann McConnell. In the Pontins Ladies' Championship in 1981 Mandy Fisher made a 37 break in a very tense stage of the final in which she beat Sue Foster. Male league players wouldn't mind making breaks like that!

Canada's Mary Ann McConnell. Photo: John Carty.

As they acquire more match experience and associate more with the world's leading professionals, women snooker players are certain to improve still further. Each year brings a batch of new Canadians, who have been like a blast of fresh air to the game with their policy of attack and attack again. But it seems unlikely that any woman will improve to the point where she could qualify for the Embassy World Championship and do well at the Crucible. Theoretically, if a woman had all the advantages of training and opportunity to play that are available to a man, there is no reason why a woman should not play as well as a man. Strength is not required; women have sufficient stamina; yet somehow they do not produce the consistent skills of male players. This, however, is true of tennis, golf and other sports, but women can still be stars playing against other women. No one would claim, for example, that Billie Jean King could beat Bjorn

Borg, but in her own arena she has beaten everyone else. Women's snooker could progress in the same way as tennis – and there are a lot of wealthy girls in that sport!

Sadly, as everything seems to be coming into place for the women in the world of snooker, the most distinguished lady player of them all, the most successful professional woman player ever, Joyce Gardner of London, died in August 1981. Joyce was seven times a winner of the English billiards title and four times a finalist in the snooker. She had a highest break of 82 at snooker and of 318 in billiards. She was a friend of Joe Davis and played him and all the other great names in the game on countless occasions in exhibition matches.

For much of her career Joyce arranged snooker exhibitions for charities and in the sixties and early seventies her charity circuit was one of the few means of getting professional players into the clubs. For a time it seemed as if clubs would not book professional snooker players unless it was for a good cause. This may have been a mistaken impression as no one could monitor all exhibitions played in small clubs around the country, but it is true to say that Joyce's efforts, as well as raising thousands of pounds for charity, helped to keep exhibition snooker alive in its darkest days. Matches arranged by her were a welcome stepping-stone for aspiring young professionals like Graham Miles and Dennis Taylor. She was a fine player, a great entertainer and a very gracious lady. Her work on behalf of charities was rewarded with Life Governorships of the Royal Northern Hospital and the Royal Infant Orphanage. She was delighted with the modern revival of the women's game and urged the players to play as she used to – attractively.

Further development of the women's world of snooker will come from the birth, in 1981, of a new women's association, the World Ladies' Billiards and Snooker Association. There had been some dissent within the membership of the original assocation run by Walter West, giving rise to the sort of in-fighting which is unfortunately all too common within the politics of amateur snooker. The new organization was the brainchild of broadcaster Peter Scowcroft, who is a director of the marketing and promotions company Grocer Jack. Peter has access to major companies with thousands of pounds of sponsorship money at their disposal and he has plans to promote the women's game in a very big way. Most of the top women players joined the new association and two hundred members had signed up within weeks of its announcing its existence.

Whether the new association will absorb the old one or continue as a separate entity was unclear as 1981 drew to a close. What was clear was that the promotional skills of the new organization and the funds of its clients, like Guinness and Beecham, will give the women's game the most efficient and lucrative set-up they have ever had. Women have obvious attractions for sponsors – they not only buy more things but, if we are to believe the advertising experts, they persuade men to buy too. There are many companies who could not readily 'fit in' with male snooker but who would feel that women's snooker was just right for their image. Thus the women players will attract new money into the game and not merely take a share of what is already available. It will be a lot of money. The first attractive young woman who can make century breaks regularly will earn at least £50,000 a year. Nice work if you can get it, but isn't it unfair? No one ever specified that Terry Griffiths, Cliff Thorburn and Steve Davis had to be both young and attractive (although no doubt they are) – but for a woman player, these are thought to be essential qualities. Unfair it is, unfair it will remain, but perhaps at £50,000 a year our leading lady might learn to put up with it.

15
Snooker stars

Many people profess to be sceptical about astrology, but it is rare to find someone who doesn't know their own star sign. Whether you believe in it or not, it can provide a lot of interesting statistics. For example, it's surprising how many Pisceans and Cancerians there are in the nursing profession. Your local bank manager is more likely to be a Taurean than anything else. Leos, with all their sense of drama, make good actors and directors. Anything analytical or involving attention to detail, such as accountancy, is best handled by Virgos.

But what about the snooker world? There is not enough data at this stage to draw any firm conclusions, but it appears that snooker holds a fascination for water signs. In the professional game there is a fair mixture of star signs but the amateur game provides clear evidence that the water signs predominate. Curiously, the man generally rated first and foremost among snooker players, Joe Davis, was an Aries, though there have been and are very few other Arians at the top of the game. Not only players follow the pattern – at a recent big professional tournament it was found that four of the top six journalists present were born under water signs: Sidney Friskin of *The Times*, a Piscean; Ted Corbett of the *Daily Star*, also a Piscean; Terry Smith of the *Daily Mirror*, a Cancerian; and Alastair Ross of the *Sun*, a Scorpio.

A recent survey of three big amateur tournaments also showed that water signs ruled the roost on all three occasions. In each event there were sixty-four entrants, so everyone had a chance. In the first tournament there were, among the last sixteen runners, six water signs, the other ten being split between earth, air and fire. The second and third events had no fewer than ten water signs each among the last sixteen competitors: five Pisces, four Cancers and one Scorpio. By the time the final of each tournament arrived, only water signs were left – in the first Pisces v Pisces, and in the other two Pisces v Cancer. In all three cases the winner was a different person, and every one was Piscean: Roy Connor, Dene O'Kane and the classiest amateur in England, Bob Harris. Perhaps the great Alex Higgins, the most successful Piscean in snooker, started this trend.

Jimmy Wych

SUN SIGN: CAPRICORN (goat)
QUALITY: CARDINAL
ELEMENT: EARTH
ASCENDANT: ARIES (ram)

Photo: Dave Muscroft.

Capricorns are ambitious, serious and methodical in thought, with a well-developed ability to concentrate. Outwardly calm and somewhat detached, they are usually very status-conscious. Jimmy's sun is placed in the tenth house of career which also rules ambition and business areas. He will have a desire for recognition and the ability to rise through his own efforts. Many politicians have this placement, which marks them for positions of responsibility. As far as his career is concerned,

Jimmy will be able to endure many setbacks and will be power-driven to succeed in some way because achieving his ambitions will be very important to him.

Moon in Aries will make him self-assertive and he will gain prominence through perseverance. This moon placement often produces emotionally impulsive natures, tempers which can flare up suddenly but temporarily. Jimmy will be pretty independent and will prefer to follow his own path of action (right or wrong) and will not readily accept interference from others. Moon in the twelfth house of the subconscious is often indicative of someone who likes to dwell in the world of imagination. It usually denotes some difficulty in expressing emotions and they are therefore kept inside. This reluctance to communicate feelings is usually tied in with past experiences and often results in shyness and feelings that are easily hurt. Jimmy has Mercury in Capricorn and therefore he will try to be logical and practical and will have a serious outlook on life. That's not to say he can't be witty when the mood takes him. He will be conservative and realistic more often than idealistic, but he must guard against melancholy! In the house of career this will mean more than one occupation, and he would be well suited to public life where he can communicate with the media.

Venus in Capricorn normally means a sincere, conventional nature in matters of affection, although there is a tendency to be too serious and controlled, often calculating and always striving for perfection. While reserved (and probably repressing emotions) in public, Jimmy will be very different in private. He will be loyal and steadfast to those close to him. Yet another planet in his career house will add strength to his ambitions, but Venus will provide a little diplomacy to his determination and will not therefore bring unpopularity with his success.

Mars in Scorpio will lend energy to Jimmy's ambitions and could cause him to be critical of others as well as himself. He must learn self-discipline in order to be constructive. He will have a quiet kind of courage when faced with difficulties and the unusual quality of being unafraid of death. There will be a Scorpionic tendency towards secrecy and he will not reveal future plans without good reason. Mars in the house of relationships will help him to be independent, enterprising and combative in relations with others. Unfortunately, Mars in the seventh house often causes these people to commit themselves too seriously and too early to a steady relationship which does not last as they anticipated. And it hurts.

Jupiter-in-Gemini people are usually broad-minded, mentally alert and talkative – when it suits them. They can also be superficial – when it suits them. It's not unusual for them to be attracted to travel and literature. They also show an interest in philosophy, education and law. Many seek a university training, but even without this their mental curiosity can lead them to be intellectually advanced without formal education. Jimmy has a combination in his second house of money which suggests he has business ability and should find a way to financial success one way or another. He will appreciate tangible assets but must take care not to be extravagant and waste what he accumulates. Snooker is only one way of making money; other avenues to success are real estate, education, travel and work in any kind of institution.

Saturn in Scorpio suggests that a shrewd and sometimes secretive mental attitude will be seen in the subject. He will be obstinate on occasions. There will be a deep need for emotional release which, if ignored, will bring about melancholy. Unexplained phenomena could possibly stir up curiosity in the occult. Though not normally one to hold a grudge, Jimmy is capable of harbouring deep resentment if dealt with unjustly. Again, this seventh house placement suggests a disappointment in an early relationship which will put off the final commitment to marriage until a later age than usual. If and when the step is taken, it is very often to an older partner.

Uranus in Cancer shows a love of home and country, but Jimmy has an unfortunate combination in his fourth house of home, roots and family. Cancer is in its natural house but Uranus signifies upheaval. It indicates that he has experienced a disruptive home life, probably at an early age. People with this placement often end up with certain hang-ups and can be emotionally unstable. However, if they channel their concentration into some inner soul-searching, they can overcome these problems. Because people of this nature resent over-strict parental control, they often leave home to seek the freedom that family life did not allow. This in turn triggers off a need for security and often results in feelings of rebelliousness and sudden mood changes. It often also leads to many changes of residence.

People with Neptune in the seventh house are usually charming and sensitive, enjoying platonic relationships. They like and need companionship, but sometimes find it difficult to judge the motives of those they meet. This often leads to unusual friendships and frequently indicates Karmic (relating to 'past lives') or psychic links within their partnerships. They often have artistic or musical talents or at the very least have a deep appreciation of them.

With Pluto in the sixth house of health, it would be quite natural for Jimmy to be interested in diet, hygiene, keeping fit and good health in general. Capricorns' physiological weaknesses are usually knees, a tendency to skin disorders, and the skeletal system. The digestive system can also suffer owing to over-acidity, worry and the suppression of emotions.

Jimmy's ascendant is Aries (fire) which should make him frank, open, often outspoken and, of course, ambitious. He could be fiery-tempered when pushed, but once he has said his piece he will forget it. He will have power, energy and aggression when needed. Altogether a pretty determined character, not to be taken lightly under any circumstances – he means business.

Tony Knowles

SUN SIGN: GEMINI (twins)
QUALITY: MUTABLE
ELEMENT: AIR
ASCENDANT: VIRGO (virgin)

Photo: John Carty.

Tony has his sun in Gemini and therefore we are not just looking at one personality – or even two, as the symbol suggests – because these characters are so changeable, one sometimes wonders just how many people they have in that one body. Geminis are versatile, restless, talkative and often contradictory. They are therefore difficult to understand and keep up with. No sooner have you fallen into step with them than you find they've changed the dance. And this is exactly what Geminis can do – lead you a fine old dance. With sun in the tenth house of career, Tony will have both the desire and the ability to reach the top of his, providing he keeps his dynamo in good working order.

Moon in Pisces creates a vivid imagination, often poetical or musical, but it also tends to cause psychological instability. Although sympathetic and gentle-natured, moon-in-Pisces people are prone to tremendous mood changes, are easily hurt and sometimes develop a persecution complex. These people usually have an awful lot to say for themselves, but what people don't realize (including the subjects themselves) is that all this chatter is often a cover-up for inner feelings of inferiority. It would help if a more realistic outlook on life were adopted. In the seventh house this pairing will have the effect of making the subject status-conscious and will give a strong desire for social success. This moon position indicates that he will be protective towards his chosen mate, but for some reason moody partners are often attracted. It also indicates that marriage is often influenced by the family.

Mercury in Gemini confirms that Tony is curious, quick-thinking, and probably highly strung. Although these people often suffer from inner confusion, they are able to communicate well and can certainly get on with most people at a superficial level. They sometimes appear impersonal because they seem more concerned with facts than personal attitudes. Because of their highly sensitive nervous system they have many changes of mind. In order not to spread themselves too thinly they should try to concentrate in one direction at a time. People with this combination in the career house are often attracted to public or business life and have the ability to deal with it. Their careers are rarely accidental but are deliberately chosen to reach specific goals. These goals usually entail communication with the public and they are usually good at speechmaking.

Venus in Taurus shows that Tony is capable of deep emotions and has artistic talents with the possibility of a good singing voice. He will appreciate possessions and therefore would like his home to be one of luxury as well as comfort. He will be a good host. He will be a little self-indulgent in areas like clothes and will never say no to a good meal. Personal beauty will be important – he will work at being clean and attractive to look at. Usually conservative in dress, these people appreciate expensive or at least good-looking clothes and even when dressed casually still look smart. There will be (although Tony will probably deny it) a kinship with the earth – with flowers, trees, plants and natural beauty. Placement in the ninth house will add a touch of class and a dash of idealism. Tony can be sympathetic and charming when he wants to be. He would rather be busy than idle, so he'll keep occupied and on the move. You can tell when a Gemini is bored or restless: if he's sitting with his legs crossed, watch his foot – it starts bobbing up and down slowly then becomes more agitated until in the end he has to jump up to find something to do.

Having Mars in Cancer must be like having a bomb in the house, Mars representing war and energy and Cancer representing the home. On the one hand the subject will be emotional, sensitive, sensuous and seeking security; on the other hand he will be moody, ambitious and tenacious. These changes can cause discord, but if the subject represses his anger it can lead to ulcers or nervous stomach upsets. Mars in Cancer can also indicate interest in the supernatural and, believe it or not, a sneaking interest in home improvements and DIY.

Mars in the tenth house tells us that Tony would prefer to be his own boss and doesn't care much for being told what to do or receiving advice, because he's almost certain to think that he knows best anyway. This attitude could cause a problem with a parent, but with all that courage and energy there will be no stopping him.

Tony has Jupiter in Leo so it follows that he will often be dramatic and creative and will like prestige. He should be generous, popular and enjoy parties and social occasions. He will have confidence and a certain dignity too. This, however, can also bring about conceit and rarely contributes to a small ego! It would be wise for all Jupiter-Leo people to learn that greatness is achieved and is not a natural right, but once this is understood and accepted they deserve to be liked and admired. It is possible for them to make money from entertainment, sport, art and education, but they are often over-optimistic when faced with speculation and prone to take risks because they get a great buzz from a gamble.

Jupiter in the eleventh house of friendship often proves to be lucky as the subjects tend to have helpful friends and an active social life which lends itself to business contacts. This combination stresses that business success will come through fraternal organizations.

Neptune in Libra produces charming, refined people who can handle many platonic friendships. Neptune is the planet of illusion and escapism, so care must be taken against deception. Its placement in the second house indicates that money is earned in an unusual way. Tony will be capable of high earnings, but must guard against spending them in a frivolous way. He must learn to budget.

Pluto in the twelfth house of the subconscious can cause hyper-sensitivity, emotional tension and occasional jealousy. The key to these problems is to look deep inside and learn to understand yourself in relation to the outside world. Be totally honest, then come to terms with yourself.

Any physiological weaknesses will be shown in the respiratory or nervous systems. There may be a tendency to pulmonary disorders such as bronchitis, pleurisy or asthma, and possibly trouble with the sciatic nerves.

Geminis are associated with air and lungs and it is quite normal for them to produce a volume of words. As the Irish have their blarney, so the Geminis have their 'patter'. However, in Tony's case his Gemini traits will be influenced by Virgo on his ascendant (an earth sign but also ruled by Mercury). Virgo should have a stabilizing effect, bring a little modesty and add sensitivity towards other people. Other Virgoan features could show themselves too, such as paying a great deal of attention to detail, being very analytical and indeed critical, and being fastidious and as near to being a perfectionist as possible.

Graham Miles

SUN SIGN: TAURUS (bull)
QUALITY: FIXED
ELEMENT: EARTH
ASCENDANT: SCORPIO (scorpion)

Taureans are by nature purposeful, practical and easy-going people. They are not easily provoked but can be furious when eventually aroused. Money will be important, not for its own sake but because it brings security and that is high on their priority list. Money is a means of providing a home, which is also important, a tangible possession and anchor. An 'ideal home' is not necessary, but it would by choice be in good taste with an air of luxury and, above all, comfort. Money also represents paid bills. Taureans do not like the worry of outstanding debts. It also buys possessions, not for showing off but as another form of security.

Graham will no doubt be endowed with the usual Taurean willpower and strength of endurance. He will almost certainly be practical, resourceful,

Photo: Dave Muscroft.

conservative, and at times stubborn. Because they like to be sure of their future, Taureans plan ahead and don't believe in 'live for today and worry about tomorrow when it gets here'. They like to know where they're going, when, how and why, and once it's settled in their minds they don't like having to change their plans.

Sun in Taurus in the marriage and partnership house indicates success in marriage, which is just as well because it will be of paramount importance. It is indicative that the subject will attract not only a strong, loyal marriage partner of enduring affection, but also close and loyal friendships that will last for years.

The moon placement shows clear financial fluctuations. It also tells us that, although outwardly reserved and self-reliant, the inner person is emotionally charged and takes personal matters very seriously. There can be instances of moodiness or tactless remarks – even the odd bout of secrecy – but in general Graham will be open-natured with a good sense of humour. He will have a practical, logical mind and will normally take care in expressing his thoughts. He will dislike arguments but will fight to protect his security and financial interests. Most Taureans learn best by visual demonstration rather than by reading or hearing about it. Although normally slow to learn, once they have grasped knowledge it will never be forgotten.

Mercury is placed in the seventh house which means that Graham will have no trouble in communicating and he should get on especially well with young people. It is not uncommon for marriage to be with a co-worker, employee or relative. People with Mercury in the seventh house should be careful when signing contracts.

Venus in Taurus tells us that Graham is a gentle, affectionate, sociable man who has a strong love of music. This placing confirms pleasant manners and consideration for others. These people are usually successful in psychology, sales and public relations. Their major successes come in marriage and partnerships.

Although Taureans are basically steady, dependable people, Mars in Aquarius shows a desire to be not only independent, but also to pursue an unusual or unorthodox course of action sometimes. It also indicates enterprise and a certain amount of impatience. Mars in this sign signifies a detached outlook. Once the subject has achieved security, he likes the freedom to come and go as he pleases. Another Aquarian effect would be an interest in reforms and good causes. It can also stir an interest in electronic, mechanical or engineering fields, and because of the Aquarian influence this interest often comes to fruition via a humanitarian channel, an example of the result of such a combination being the invention of the motorized wheelchair. Aquarian-influenced subjects will also be good at updating traditional methods, their attitude being that tradition should only be respected when it deserves to be. Consequently they do not find it easy to work under authoritarian direction. They should be allowed to do things their own way and learn from their own mistakes. This is all quite foreign to the run-of-the-mill Taurean.

Mars in the fourth house of home means difficulties regarding either the home itself or parents. Of course, the energy can come out in other ways – it could mean that Graham is (time permitting) a mad-keen handyman who puts lots of energy into home repairs or building cupboards and so on. Mars can have other effects regarding housing: if it is well aspected it means land or buildings may be inherited, but if badly aspected it may mean loss regarding a house, garage or land. The loss would usually arise by fire, theft or tax problems concerning that property.

Jupiter puts a fourth planet in Taurus. Again this

tell us that Graham is good-hearted, usually reliable, and has sound judgment. He needs the comfort of home and loves good food and drink. Because he enjoys material success he runs the risk of being greedy, but if wisdom and discrimination in investing money are developed it can be used in the most constructive way. Jupiter-in-Taurus people can envisage and carry out enterprises on a large scale over a long period of time, though occasionally they may over-reach themselves financially without sufficient collateral to meet unforeseen contingencies. The seventh house again indicates success in marriage and that the subject would be attracted to a professional partner such as a teacher or someone of intellectual standing. This combination indicates an open, friendly person with a strong sense of justice. Because they try to be fair and honest, they expect others to be the same. Unfortunately Jupiter can leave them vulnerable to charlatans and people with grandiose ideas without the backing to see them through.

Saturn indicates that Graham will have to work hard to earn the security he needs. It also signifies caution and the will to function under pressure. About the age of twenty-nine is when these Jupiter-Taurus people really start putting their backs into their domestic, financial and career ambitions, and since they are frugal they start to save for emergencies and old age. Saturn is also in the seventh house and it has the uncanny knack of delaying marriage for some reason. As well as holding things up, it quite often entails other responsibilities. Saturn in this house can sometimes be the cause of treachery or law suits brought by an enemy.

Uranus in Taurus gives an inner strength to bulldoze through problems. Uranus in the seventh house can be responsible for sudden changes of mood, opinion or attitude in an otherwise stable personality.

Neptune in Virgo gives an analytical approach to religious matters. Although Taureans are usually healthy, Neptune in Virgo can sometimes manifest itself in a tendency to psychosomatic illnesses. Although the subject is capable of flashes of intuition, he often doubts their validity and will not act upon them. Neptune in the eleventh house of friendship will have the effect of attracting strange or unusual friends.

Pluto in Leo indicates involvement in a power struggle. Placed in the ninth house of high ideals, it shows an urge to reform and regenerate. The subject will be able to sense fundamental causes of problems and gain an insight into the future. He will have little tolerance of hypocrisy and social injustice. If he feels that existing institutions are unworthy of respect, he may become a revolutionary.

16

The teenage revolution

A continuing feature of snooker in 1981 was that the average age of players went on falling. While Jimmy White was once a rarity in making century breaks at the age of sixteen, century breaks by such young players are now quite commonplace; where he was virtually unique in turning professional as a teenager, this is no longer unusual and we now have professionals like Dean Reynolds and Tommy Murphy.

There are many reasons for this increase in juvenile talent. There are more incentives for them to play well and it is not unknown for a sixteen-year-old to pick up prizes of £150 or £200. There are more opportunities for them to play, too. Many clubs, particulary the snooker centres, now allow young people to be full members, and if the boys have adequate access to a table it is bound to increase their skills. With table charges in the South of England now at £2 per hour – and the rest of the country not far behind – one welcome trend is that club owners help to develop the talents of the youngsters by allowing them free table time. There are now so many good snooker centres around Britain that the best of the young brigade can find one close at hand which will offer them this arrangement. It is good for the youngster because he cannot afford to pay the costs of perhaps twenty hours' snooker each week, and it is good for the club because the members can take a pride in 'their' boy, watch him play or play against him.

The economic depression in Britain, with thousands of teenagers unable to find work, also has some influence on the increasing number of successful young players. If a boy is out of work he has plenty of time to spend on snooker, and if he knows that there is virtually no chance of his finding a job he need not feel guilty about spending all day in the snooker club. For some of the youngsters there are better career prospects on the table than there are at the local Jobcentre. In Britain today there are dozens of young people under the age of eighteen who are capable of making century breaks and they offer an example to still younger players to practise and improve their game. We now have regular teenage members of national teams, boys of twelve years old playing in leagues. Where will it end? Who will be the first player unable to compete in the Embassy World Championship unless he brings his mum with him? The first to retire halfway through an evening match because it's past his bedtime?

In this chapter we introduce some of the boys who have caught our eye in 1981.

Steve Ventham

Photo: John Carty.

A fifteen-year-old from Mitcham, South London, Steve Ventham grew up in the shadow of his near neighbour, Jimmy White, and is now one of the brightest young prospects in London. He has a highest break of 129 and is a regular at the Top Spot Club, Balham, South London. He hit the newspaper headlines in 1981 when the local education authority had a row with his parents regarding his attendance at school. His headmaster had allowed him afternoons off to practise snooker, but the school alleged that Steve was taking mornings and afternoons off – five days a week! Steve's mother and father support his snooker ambitions strongly and while they contended that he had kept to the school agreement, they have no doubts on one point: 'His snooker comes first.'

Jerry Williams

Sixteen-year-old Jerry Williams from Balham, South London, is the first of the West Indian Britons to lay claim to real potential as a top snooker player. The game is very popular with all immigrant communities around the country, and it is to be expected that West London or Yorkshire will soon produce a genuine contender from among their Indian or Pakistani players. Jerry himself is British-born and he is managed by Bob Davis, the man who first brought Tony Meo and Jimmy White to prominence. Jerry has made many century breaks and he enters every tournament he can find in order to gain experience. That policy paid off in October 1981 when Jerry won his first senior tournament, the Midland Bank Competition at Colchester, Essex, taking a first prize of £175 from quite a strong field. Although the tournament was handicapped, Jerry received only 14 points start and had to work hard for his first big win. There will be others.

Chris Hamson

In 1981 fifteen-year-old Chris Hamson of Nottingham won the British Under-16s Championship and this title has proved to be a stepping-stone for many of today's best-known names. Chris is another young man who will travel anywhere to compete in a tournament and he was unlucky to lose to Terry Whitthread, the eventual winner, when he reached the semi-final of the World Junior Championship at the Guinness Festival of Snooker in May 1981. He is a regular player at Kingston Snooker Centre in Surrey, where Cliff Thorburn and Kirk Stevens practise, having moved to the area specifically to improve his snooker.

Paul Ennis

A nineteen-year-old from Dublin, Paul Ennis is keeping alive the tradition that the Irish will always be strongly represented among the best snooker players. He was Irish Boys' Champion in 1978 and runner-up in the Irish Youth Championship (losing to John Kearney) in 1979. He was trained at the Home of Billiards Club in Dublin by leading Irish amateur Richie Dunne, and has many big breaks to his credit, the highest being a 142. When he left school he was accepted for training as a jockey at the famous school at the Curragh, but he soon grew too heavy to have any future in that direction and now concentrates on snooker.

Terry Whitthread (left) with Paul Ennis. Photo: John Carty.

THE TEENAGE REVOLUTION

Paul followed the well-trodden path to London and now plays at the Ron Gross Centre. In 1981 he won the London Junior Championship and followed this up with the London Senior title, beating Dave Gilbert in the final. He made his first appearance in the Irish team in 1981 and gave a good account of himself.

Terry Whitthread

Perhaps the best-known of London youngsters after Jimmy White, Terry Whitthread had a lean record of success since becoming the youngest player ever to win the London Championship in 1980. However, in May 1981 he burst back to form to win the World Junior Championship at the Isle of Wight. This championship was not officially organized in the way that the senior World Amateur Championship is arranged, with affiliated countries sending one or two official representatives; it was organized on an 'open' basis, so that any young person could enter, and it was said to be recognized by the B&SCC. Some of the best young players in the world took part, including Dene O'Kane from New Zealand and Greg Jenkins from Australia, so Terry's win cannot be devalued too much by doubts about its official status. Even in today's conditions it is unlikely that the various national bodies could afford to send young players to a championship organized on the lines of the World Amateur. None of this will trouble young Terry too much. He won, and that's what counts. All he wants now is to win everything else.

John Parrott

This young player from Liverpool has, at the age of eighteen, confirmed the potential he first showed in 1980 when he started to make his name outside the Merseyside area. In the 1981 English Championship John had an excellent run, beating Bill Kelly and Dennis Hughes, two of the very top amateurs who are now professionals, before losing to Ian Williamson of Leeds. Throughout 1981 he showed consistently improving form and gained useful experience in a series of exhibition matches with Dean Reynolds. In the Pontins Open Championship in October 1981 he beat Les Dodd, England international player and recognized as top amateur in Liverpool, and reached the quarter-finals of this tournament (which had 650 entrants), losing to another of England's best senior men, John Hargreaves of Stoke. John Parrott's progress is sensibly monitored and encouraged by his father and he clearly has a bright future ahead.

Neal Foulds

Eighteen-year-old Londoner Neal Foulds has been a lad of some promise since he was fourteen, but it was not clear if he was just keeping his dad Geoff happy or if he had a real appetite for the game. He has now proved beyond doubt that he is a young man of genuine talent who may one day overshadow his better-known father. His style is markedly different from his dad's in that he plays an attacking

John Parrott. Photo: Dave Muscroft.

Neal Foulds. Photo: John Carty.

game of the kamikaze school. His most outrageous power shots should lead him into terrible trouble, but in fact they tend to work out very well. He won the London Junior Championship in 1980 and made his debut at county level with the London under-23 team. Such has been his progress that in 1981 he was selected for the London senior team. When he left school early in 1981 he took a job in an insurance office but 'retired' after three months to become a full-time player under the management of former professional Ron Gross. He was Riley Intermediate Champion of London and the Home Counties in 1981, and in November won a big open tournament at Pot Black, Plymouth, beating Les Dodd in the final. With the departure of father Geoff to the professional ranks it seems likely that young Neal will ensure that the Foulds name stays at the forefront of London amateur snooker, where it has been for ten years.

Paddy Browne

Paddy Browne of Phibsborra near Dublin is another seventeen-year-old from Ireland who combines a deadly ability on the table with that infectious smile which is the speciality of the Irish. The game can get a bit too serious and intense, even in the junior ranks, and it is always nice to see a young man who can come away from a defeat with a big smile and the attitude that tomorrow is another day. Paddy gets most of his practice against Irish Professional Eugene Hughes and he had the temerity to make his lifetime best break of 141 in a game against Eugene! Paddy's talents were recognized when he was capped for Ireland in 1981.

Paddy Browne.

Michael Gold

Twelve-year-old Michael Gold from Exeter is as far as we're prepared to go this year! He's knee-high to a half-butt and looks as if he should be playing with his Action Man rather than a 17-ounce cue. But he's good. His best break is a 56 and such is his quality that he is a regular player in the Exeter league – one of the youngest league competitors we've ever heard of. As befits a young man of such tender years, he is a great spectator of the game and very willing to learn. His father Eric is a referee and Devon amateur official, so young Michael's progress will be kept on the right lines.

17

Tony's Australian dream

It is no longer enough to be a master snooker player, to make maximum breaks, to beat people, to win titles in the amateur ranks or in the lower echelons of the professional game. There are now nearly eighty registered professional players, about half of whom are young men waiting for their first big chance. Sometimes that chance is long delayed, in some cases it never comes, but most often it comes in the qualifying rounds of a major championship and the young hopeful, soberly confronted with harsh reality, is tried and found wanting.

There is little doubt that among the new professionals there are ten or twelve players who could make it to the very top of the game – if they ever get the chance. There is equally little doubt that most of them from time to time think, 'If only Reg Perrin would phone and invite me to appear in "Pot Black",' or 'If only that one invitation would come through, the one that would get me on television and give me a chance to beat all the top professionals.' It doesn't often happen like that, even today. Ray Reardon, Fred Davis, Dennis Taylor – any of the established world stars – would smile wryly at this daydream and point to their own long years of hard and frustrating apprenticeship before they reached the top.

But for one player in 1981 *that* phone call did come through. It was in July and the Winfield Masters Tournament was being played in Sydney, Australia. It wasn't an event that was uppermost in the mind of Tony Meo as he went to the Top Spot Club, Balham, for his usual afternoon's practice – he was not one of the invited players and he'd be content to hear all about it when the others returned. Unknown to Tony, however, halfway across the world in the opposite direction one of the invited players, Kirk Stevens, found that he would be unable to go to Australia and he withdrew from the tournament. So the phone rang that afternoon in the Top Spot Club: 'Hello, Tony, Ted Lowe here. You're going to Australia in two days' time to compete in the Winfield Masters.' Tony thought it was a joke. He stood stunned, racking his brains, trying to think which one of his South London friends had the talent to mimic Ted Lowe so well. But that voice belongs to only one person. It was Ted Lowe all right. There was no question in Ted's voice. He didn't say, 'Would you like to go to Australia?' or 'Are you able to go to Australia?' Ted knew the importance of what he was offering and he knew that to offer it properly he should have a silver platter and a fanfare of trumpets, but he took a benevolent delight in hitting Tony smack between the eyes with the proposition.

There was, of course, only one answer. As Tony said later, 'If he'd said I had to go right there and then I'd have done it!' However, there were the formalities of obtaining a visa and Ted, showing all the experience of a lifetime's globetrotting, extracted the required documents from the officials at Australia House with time to spare. Two days later Tony was at Heathrow Airport, cue in hot little hand, to meet Ted and join Cliff Thorburn and Doug Mountjoy who were booked on the same flight. Tony was no stranger to international air travel, having been a star of the busy amateur

Ted Lowe in Australia. Photo: Ted Lowe Collection.

The line-up for the Winfield Masters Tournament (left to right): Eddie Charlton, Cliff Thorburn, Doug Mountjoy, Dennis Taylor, Tony Meo, John Spencer, Paddy Morgan and Ian Anderson. Photo: Ted Lowe Collection.

circuit and a sponsored competitor in professional events, but this was the longest flight he had undertaken. 'I'm not exactly one of the white-knuckle brigade,' he said. 'I don't mind flying really, but I'm not too keen on the take-off. Once we're above the clouds and levelled out I don't mind, because then it's like being in someone's living-room.'

The flight was spent, as snooker players usually spend such flights, in playing cards. 'We had seven hours to Bahrain where our stop was extended by three hours by technical problems, then eight hours to our next stop in Singapore and another seven hours to Sidney,' recalls Tony. 'It wasn't so bad – we had about ten meals each during the flight!' The captain invited Ted and Tony up to the flight deck to see how everything worked. Tony, looking at all the instruments, thought for the first time in his life that maybe snooker was really quite easy.

On arrival at Sydney Airport the party was met by Eddie Charlton and Ian Anderson, who took them to their hotel, the Commodore Chateau, one of the best in the city. There were two free days for Tony before he took part in the competition. He used them as any visitor to Australia would, in seeing all the sights. Tony had known that he was leaving the summer of London for the winter of Sydney, but he found the climate surprising. 'It was 60 or 70° and sunny – they don't know what a real winter is,' he said.

Although Tony is a well-known and popular player in the UK, he was rather an unknown quantity to the Australians and he was not surrounded by familiar faces as he would be in England. 'I wanted to do so much, but I'd have felt funny on my own,' said the gregarious Tony, 'but Ted Lowe removed all the problems. That man is different class [the highest possible compliment in Tooting]. He made sure I had something to do and see every day. He arranged a visit to Joyce Lindrum, which was interesting because she's the widow of the great Australian player Horace Lindrum, but she used to live in Tooting and the

TONY'S AUSTRALIAN DREAM

first thing she said to me was, "Hello, Tony, how's Tooting?" It really made me feel welcome and we had a great day out. If it had been left to me I wouldn't have had the nerve to ask to meet Joyce, but Ted smooths everything out.'

During the tournament all the overseas professionals were guests of the Tattersalls Gentlemens Club in Sydney, a famous centre of Australian snooker. Tony had heard that Australians could be a bit blunt and that they were not all keen on 'Pommies', but he got on well with everyone he met and soon made friends among the members of the club. 'The biggest difference that struck me was the lighting on the tables. It was much more flourescent lighting, which you hardly ever see in England, but I'd seen it before in Canada and I soon got used to it. I also noticed immediately that the pockets on the table are cut differently but I would expect that because their table fitters have been trained differently from those in Britain. Although the difference was obvious, the end result was much the same – I didn't find the pockets any easier or more difficult than in Britain,' said Tony.

One difference Tony did notice was in the food: 'Eddie Charlton told us right at the start that we should concentrate on seafood because it's the best in the world. I did have one steak, which was excellent, but the rest of the time I gorged myself on all this fantastic fish – stuff I'd never heard of like John Dory and red snapper. It was out of this world.'

Eddie, the undisputed king of Australian snooker, took them out to see the sights of his beloved Sydney and Tony was suitably impressed with the world-famous Opera House, 'but I didn't go inside.' For a fledgling professional, a night out with the other players and the sort of people they mix with can be a hair-raising experience. They don't eat in hamburger joints, and at a table of fourteen there is probably no one who earns less than £50,000 a year. The bill for a 'quiet dinner' of this kind can be an education in itself. 'This was where Eddie was so organized,' said Tony. 'When

Eddie Charlton. Photo: Dave Muscroft.

Tony Meo. Photo: Dave Muscroft.

we first arrived he insisted that we see all the best places but he said, "I'll divide the expenses between all of you and have them deducted from your final cheques so that you don't notice it," and he did. For eight days we lived like kings and although a deduction was made at the end, it didn't seem to be very much.'

And so to the tournament itself. The Winfield Masters is primarily a television tournament staged for the ABC channel, and it is of equal stature to the British 'Pot Black' series which is also shown in Australia. The difference in this tournament was that all points counted, rather than frames won.

The tournament was played at the Tattersalls Club, where Tony had put in some practice. 'I met some of the top Australian amateurs like John Campbell, Warren King and Greg Jenkins,' he said 'and of course as Warren and Greg have been over to the UK I knew them slightly anyway.' He also met Australia's top referee and the man who officiated in all the televized matches, Ron Tscherney: 'A wonderful man and a wonderful referee,' Tony declared.

At this stage of the trip the biggest thrill for Tony was to meet the great Australian player Murt O'Donoghue. Murt was the first man to make a 147 break in snooker (in 1934) – before Joe Davis or anyone else. Tony is keenly aware that he is the youngest player ever to have made the maximum break and he was not unconscious of the historical significance of their meeting: the first and the youngest, with more than fifty years between their ages. Tony says, 'He must be over eighty, but he's as fit as a fiddle and never stops laughing. I think he's great. He gave me a lot of advice and encouragement and you can be sure I listened to everything he had to say.'

With the tournament under way, Tony scored a good win over John Spencer but lost to Australia's Ian Anderson. He narrowly defeated Doug Mountjoy of Wales and reached the semi-final because of his high tally of points scored. In his semi-final against Cliff Thorburn, Tony made breaks of 68 and 82 for a good win but, as he admits, 'I got away with a few bad mistakes in my match against Cliff.' After each match Tony had a chat with Murt O'Donoghue and after the Thorburn match the Australian doyen was uncompromising: 'Not good enough,' he told Tony. 'Your safety play must be improved.'

Tony took this advice to heart and in the final he beat John Spencer, the holder of the title, by 319 points to 84 in the three-frame aggregate match. The line-up for this event had included some of the world's best players: Thorburn, Taylor, Charlton, Spencer, Morgan, Mountjoy, Anderson. The young man from South London, on his first appearance in Australia, had come out on top for a lucrative and satisfying win.

Having started as a relatively unknown newcomer, Tony now had Australia at his feet. 'The spectators knew about me from the programme notes and I had the usual autograph requests,' said Tony, 'but when I won it they all went mad and couldn't clap and cheer me enough. It was great. The funny thing was that as soon as the organizers had known that I was taking part, they slanted all their publicity about me on the fact that I was so young. By British standards I'm no longer young. Even Jimmy White isn't a teenager now. When you look at all the new youngsters coming up, you can't say that Jimmy and I are 'young' – but, of course, in Australian eyes we are. Anyway, I was to be presented on television interviews and so on as a 'boy wonder' and the producers had a fright when they saw me. The problem is that I'm a bit of a 'bluebeard' and have to shave at least twice a day – I get a five o'clock shadow at noon! But I shaved four times a day and the make-up girls spent an hour on me each time before I went in front of the cameras, so I don't think I looked too ancient!'

Taking account of his prize and the fact that all expenses of the trip had been covered, Tony earned about 5,000 dollars for the week. This was his highest-earning week, because when the dollars

On his triumphant return from Australia, Tony signed with a new manager, Barry Hearn. Photo: Cue World.

were converted in the UK the exchange rate had altered dramatically – in his favour – and the Australian win exceeded the proceeds of his week in the Courage English Championship when he had earned £2,000 for reaching the final. Tony said, 'I spent about 600 dollars when I was out there, but that was on presents for my wife Denise and my daughter Gina. I bought Gina a big koala bear. Apart from the presents, I never had to put my hand in my pocket. This was another thing I noticed about Ted Lowe when we went round the shops – how thoughtful he is. He must have sent over thirty postcards to family and friends back home; I had a struggle to send one. When we were in the shops I learned just how highly Ted Lowe is rated in Australia – our tournament hadn't been shown yet, but everywhere we went, as soon as Ted asked the shop assistants for something they'd say, "I know that voice – you're Ted Lowe from the snooker!" He's like a god in Australia.'

Tony, flying home as the winner of a major Australian tournament, had cause enough to be pleased. Perhaps the most important thing, for a young man who knows that he's going to reach the very top but doesn't know quite when, were the words of Australian king-pin Eddie Charlton: 'You've won Australia, Tony. Next time you come out here for a tournament, I can fix you up with bookings for a month before the tournament begins!'

Ted Lowe knew what he was doing when he lifted that telephone. Tony Meo was tried and found winning. To quote another man in another place: he came, he saw – and he conquered.

18
Don't shoot the referee

In a match like the final of the Embassy World Championship there are two players fighting for direct prize money of some £35,000, and the winner of this encounter will earn another £150,000 as a result of his victory. The two finalists are at the top of their profession, have worked mightily to reach their present position and have maintained an astonishing level of concentration for the two weeks of the championship. So has the other participant in this match, the one no one notices: the referee.

For a fee of about £50 a day plus expenses the referee will be subject to the greatest pressures the game can provide, and if he performs very well his presence will be virtually unnoticed – that is the hallmark of a good referee. Let him make one mistake and he will find himself in a maelstrom of controversy with nothing to assist him and no support to draw upon except his own self-belief and reputation. It is in many ways a rewarding career, but it is also one of the most thankless jobs in snooker.

Alex Higgins, the scourge of referees, a player whose incidental mission in life seems to be to make young referees flinch and old referees older, has said, 'There isn't what I would call a professional referee in the game – that's why there are so many mistakes. I think referees are more susceptible to making mistakes than the players.'

This view inspires reactions from referees varying from amusement to apoplexy. They are the first to admit that they're human and make mistakes, but their response to the Higgins criticism can be distilled into the following reasonable retort: during the average frame of top-level snooker each player will fail on two pots, play one shot of the wrong strength and run out of position once or twice. If he's unlucky, he may go in-off. Are these not mistakes? The player who makes no mistakes in a frame makes a 147 break, or at least a total clearance. Any referee can put his hand on his heart and say, 'If I made as many mistakes in a frame as the players do – say an average of five between them – I'd be run out of the business!' Of course this defensive argument from the referees is partial and too rigorously logical, but it is prompted by what they consider to be partial and illogical reasoning on the part of Alex Higgins.

In general the efforts of the referees are much appreciated by the professional players and few of them would subscribe to Higgins's comments. Every player has suffered from bad decisions at some time in his career. Every player can quote 'horror stories' of just how bad a referee *can* be. But the standard has improved greatly in recent years.

In passing, one story can be quoted to show just how bad a referee can be. One leading professional tells the tale of a match in the English Championship in his amateur days. He was one of the top seeds in the area draw and was expected to win his second-round match against an unknown player who was of quite good league standard. The seeded player (we shall call him Cyril) was obviously better than his opponent, but the opponent was able to 'tie him up' and generally make life difficult. Whenever Cyril missed a pot, the referee would say, 'Come on, Cyril, I don't believe it – you can do better than that' or, 'My goodness, Cyril, we'll be here all day if you keep missing those!' The game progressed to the point where Cyril led by three frames to one without making any big breaks or stamping his authority on the game. To the observer it was clear that he would eventually win the rather uninteresting match fairly comfortably.

His opponent, however, was not an observer, but a young man anxious to make his name against the more distinguished player. In his mind the possibility of the score going to 3-2, then 3-3, then 4-3 in his favour was still a very real one – though not to the referee, as will become apparent. During the fifth frame Cyril moved into the lead. He was 15 points ahead and there were seven reds left on the table. His opponent played valiantly, but to little effect. Cyril potted the next red, took a colour, missed the next red. The next time Cyril potted a red the referee took it from the pocket (which was hardly over-full) and put it, not in an empty pocket, *but in its box on the side table*. The match went on scrappily, with Cyril potting the odd red and going further in front. And each time he potted a red the referee took it away and put it in its box, clearly indicating that this was the last frame of the match. It is not recorded what the opponent thought of this, but it is difficult to imagine any action by a

Gus Lilygreen referees during the Welsh Professional Championship. Photo: John Carty.

referee which could so obviously involve bias, pre-judgment of the result and the complete and utter demoralization of the opponent. An unhappy tale, but one with a just ending – of the three spectators in the room, two were local area officials: the referee concerned never passed beyond the 'C' grade and never refereed another official match.

Fortunately, the standard of refereeing in Britain is generally much higher than this and the real 'bad egg' does not long survive the system of grading, assessment and examination. This system is controlled by the B&SCC (Billiards & Snooker Control Council) and anyone can become a snooker referee by applying to their local association for an examination (the address of your local association can be obtained from the B&SCC, 32 John William Street, Huddersfield, Yorks). The council, in their useful handbook, have laid down the criteria for referees at each level – and it must be remembered that even the most exalted professional referee owes his qualification to the B&SCC certificate. The newcomer starts by obtaining a 'C' grade certificate and the B&SCC lays down that referees worthy of this must have 'satisfied the examiner of their knowledge of the rules, but fail in other respects: quickness of application, lack of experience, etc. They are considered to be qualified to referee matches of league-importance, but not championship matches promoted by local associations.' The 'C' grade test is not difficult provided that the applicant has studied the rules. There used to be a great fondness among examiners for asking the examinee questions on the measurements of the table – for example, the regulation height of the table (2 feet 9½ inches to 2 feet 10½ inches) or the distance of the (black) spot from the top cushion (12¾ inches). These matters are important and in fact appear at the very beginning of the General Rules, but many applicants (their heads full of theory of free balls, touching balls, outside interference and other puzzlers) have completely overlooked the regulation measurements and either fail the test or suffer some embarrassment. Their reaction to these questions is usually, 'When did you last see a referee come into the club or hall for an official match and start by checking the measurements of the table?' A good question – but many of the top referees claim that they always do so.

Bernard Franks, Secretary of the B&SCC. In addition to his other duties he issues referees' certificates and keeps track of hundreds of referees around the world.

Once applicants have obtained their 'C' certificate, their greatest need is for practical experience. They must exert themselves to officiate in any match in which the players or their association will accept them. As the amateur game has become more active in recent years, there are now many more matches in which referees may gain experience, and this is perhaps the major factor in the present-day level of expertise.

Provided that a person is fit in wit and limb there are no barriers to becoming a referee. Until 1979–80 the rules decreed that a referee had to be over twenty-one years of age. This was overdue for correction: Parliament itself had reduced the age of majority to eighteen fully ten years earlier. The London & Home Counties Association, by a process that might be described as constructive ignorance, knocked the first hole in the wall by passing the sixteen-year-old Andrew Line of Bracknell, Berks, as a 'C' grade referee in 1978. The B&SCC, when it noticed this, was obliged to consider its position. The council debated the problem. It was agreed that a limit of twenty-one was too high and a minimum age of sixteen was proposed. The council ultimately decided that there would be no minimum age limit. Under the present rules, therefore, a twelve-year-old can become a referee. Ludicrous – or is it? If snooker were well established in schools and youth organizations would it not be quite sensible to have matches between twelve-and thirteen-year-old boys and girls refereed by boys and girls of the same age? If they are intelligent and responsible, there's nothing against it. There could hardly be a better avenue into the game for boys or girls who are keen but who do not or cannot play. It could safely be left to the governing bodies to ensure that a fourteen-year-old did not become an 'A' grade referee in charge of BBC's 'Pot Black' matches.

The next step in the referee's career is the 'B' grade certificate. This can be applied for by any 'C' grade referee of more than one year's standing. According to the B&SCC handbook, 'The 'B' grade referees have satisfied the examiner that they possess a thorough knowledge of the rules combined with the ability and qualities of character and temperament necessary to apply the rules confidently and firmly in a way likely to create confidence. This class is efficient in every respect and is qualified to referee matches at any standard.'

As can be seen, this is a pretty stiff criterion, and it seems surprising that a man or woman who qualified as a 'C' grade only one year before can be so swiftly transformed into this paragon. In practice, in a well-run association, the recommendations of the examiner will be put before the commitee for approval and this ensures that only the best 'C' grade referees reach the next category. The average rate of success in one large association would indicate that the average period for which a 'C' certificate must be held before promotion is two or three years rather than one.

The precise *method* of examination for the 'B' grade is nowhere defined. Clearly it cannot be a re-hash of the 'C' grade test. Many examiners and associations consider that it must involve some observation of the referee in serious match conditions and candidates will usually be watched at work before the examination takes place. The questions at this level are not so much 'What does the rule book say?' as 'What would you do in a given set of circumstances [and there are many] where the rule book says nothing?' In this way resourcefulness, confidence and discretion are tested. The local committee debates the examiner's report before submitting an approved recommendation to the B&SCC. This is essential because the rule book mentions 'character, temperament, creating confidence' – matters upon which other officials who have seen that referee in action may have something to say. The examiner may not have noticed every characteristic of the referee while he had him or her under review. The typical reasons for rejection at this stage include: 'He wears dirty gloves'; 'He talks to the players or audience during the frame'; 'He smokes/drinks while refereeing'; 'He stands in the line of sight of the players and distracts them'. Nothing, it will be noticed, about the *rules*. But these comments, filtered through to officials from players or from their own observation, will be enough to prevent the candidate's name going forward to the B&SCC for a 'B' grade certificate. An efficient local secretary would advise the candidate of the reasons for failure and advise him or her what period of time should elapse before a further application might be successful. Any number of attempts may be made.

The top of the tree is, of course, the 'A' grade. Once again, the official B&SCC handbook sets out the position: 'The 'A' grade referees are known men (women are included) who, by experience, have proven their capabilities in conducting the highest grade of matches. They form a small select panel of specialists of exceptional merit and reputation and are selected on recommendation by promotion from the 'B' grade.' There is no examination. The 'recommendation' may come from any source but in the present day this invariably means the local association, where one exists. The promotion from 'B' to 'A' is a minefield of controversy and many hearts, friendships and indeed some associations, have broken under the stress of this appointment

DON'T SHOOT THE REFEREE

Referees assemble for the Embassy World Championship.

Referee John Williams. Photo: John Carty.

Left to right: Referees John Smyth, Len Ganley and Peter Koniotes. Photos left and centre: John Carty. Photo right: Dave Muscroft.

– or absence of it.

The first area of controversy is one that hardly appears to be open to argument: can 'B' grade referees *apply* to become an 'A' grade or must they wait in hope for the day when their local association, overwhelmed by their outstanding merit and reputation, thrust the honour upon them? It is logical to assume that if they wait in hope they'll wait forever. The people who control the local association are probably referees themselves, and referees as a breed are not usually overwhelmed by the merits of their rivals. In many cases the local officials will be 'A' grades and will loudly proclaim (once they have their own certificate) that they will not 'water down standards' by appointing just anybody. The type of official who does not want to create any new 'A' grades in his area will never, if it can be avoided, mention the subject to the prime contenders. They, in exasperation, will one day *ask* to be made up to the 'A' grade and this, so far as the hidebound official is concerned, is death to their chances of promotion because the applicant has shown 'ambition' or is 'too pushy'.

The modern, efficient association (and these are now in the majority) recognizes that some compromise must be found. In such an association it is possible for the referees to indicate that they wish to be considered for the 'A' grade without being regarded as megalomaniacs. Their letters of application are considered by the committee and much the same sort of discussion takes place as does over the 'B' grade applications. The main difference at this level is that if there is *any* well-founded criticism of the refereee, the application will fail.

The referee must hold the 'B' grade certificate for three years before appointment to the 'A' grade is possible. In fact the rule book has no comments on the subject; but there used to be so many disputes about the position that the B&SCC was obliged, some years ago, to make an 'official decision' that no one would be appointed to the 'A' grade if they had not held the 'B' certificate for at least three years. In the average case, a period of four or five years would be quite normal.

Thus our referee may have spent seven years gaining experience at all levels and taking his/her 'A' grade certificate. It is only at this stage that he/she has any real chance of appearing in a match on television in Britain because the Professional Referees Association, whose members officiate in all televized matches, recruits only 'A' grade referees.

It has been possible so far in this chapter to trace the rise of the referee from spectator in the audience to the top of the amateur class. If the path is beset with pitfalls, dense undergrowth and sniping from

Representing seventy-five years of refereeing experience, Alf Shaw (left) of Leeds and Paddy Comerford of Dublin. Photo: John Carty.

enemy quarters, it is nonetheless a path. The professional referee category may in this context be described as a brick wall – or at least a very high fence with few and exceedingly small gaps in it. In short, there is no natural progression from 'A' grade to professional. Unlike the Professional Players Association, which announces the standard to be met by anyone seeking to join their ranks, the Professional Referees Association offers no guidelines. Among their membership are some of the best referees in the country – but among those rejected there are also some of the highest ability and reputation. There would be more confidence in the PRA and less dissatisfaction in the ranks of 'amateur' referees if it were known what standards must be met to gain admission to their ranks.

It is clear that not all 'A' grade referees can become professionals. There are too many of them and some are only 'A' grades from 'rotten boroughs' or as beneficiaries of 'me too-ism' in the old days. Even within the PRA not all members have worked on television – either because their turn has not come up or the promotor of the event, doubting their ability or experience, will not have them.

In the modern world of snooker the zenith of a referee's career is a televized final. Given the importance of television, it is desirable that the best referees should have some opportunity to reach this pinnacle. As far as the public is concerned, the only known referees are those who appear on television. The best 'A' grade referee in the country who has not been on television (whoever *he* is) is known only to the committed snooker fan. To the general public he doesn't exist.

It's a long hard road to the top for any referee, whether on television or not. What makes them do it? The usual answer is 'love of the game' and indeed this must be the truth – it offers little enough in the way of other rewards. Many people decide to become referees because they want to play a part in the game and know they will never be good enough to do so as players. This is legitimate: there are those who want only to rub shoulders with Reardon, Griffiths and the like, but the long hard slog of the amateur circuit, where a word of thanks from the players is the only reward – not always given – soon sorts out the uncommitted. For those thousands whose heart is in the right place, refereeing offers an absorbing way of life, genuine respect from the snooker community and the chance to excel in a very difficult field.

When a referee makes a mistake, be it on television or at the local club, he is everyone's whipping boy and if the mistake is made in an important final it can virtually end a promising career. When a referee does a perfect job in a match he knows that half of the audience (any audience) will not appreciate the subtle skills he has shown. His progress to the top will be slower than he would wish and the peripheral 'fame' he will achieve may not be enough to warm the memory in old age. He will never get rich out of it – and most would not wish to. Throughout the game, from amateur to professional, 'C' grade to 'A', the referee is the cement of snooker, holding together a multi-million-pound sport for the price of a pint.

19

Why Steve Davis?

Steve Davis won the Embassy World Championship on 1 January 1981. That's probably not how you remember it. It's certainly not the way the record books will record it, but from about the end of that month anyone I spoke to in London or Romford – especially Romford – had Steve Davis over the line already and they merely awaited the formality of his picking up a cheque for £20,000.

In that period of anticipation before the World Championship he was the obvious man of the moment. He had had an extraordinary record of success since October when he won the Coral UK Championship. Apart from the English and Irish

Steve Davis holds aloft the cup after winning the World Championship in 1981. Photo: Dave Muscroft.

Benson & Hedges Masters, he had won every major tournament of the season. Even among the people who were not Steve Davis fans he was still the object of all speculation. While Romford was saying, 'Of course he'll win it', the supporters of other players were spending just as much time saying, 'He won't win it'. They were just as obsessed with Steve Davis, even if it was in a negative way. On my travels I was never button-holed by anyone telling me at great length that Dennis Taylor or Doug Mountjoy would or would not win it – but as soon as the name of Steve Davis came up everyone, for or against, had enough opinion and theory to put a speaker at Hyde Park Corner to shame!

Steve was the most obvious choice to win the Embassy World Championship, and at the Crucible Theatre, Sheffield, as if acting out a well-rehearsed script, he did just that.

But why Steve Davis?

I have known Steve for quite some time, since before he took his first big title, the British Boys Billiards Championship in 1975, and I have always watched his progress closely. It was always clear to me that Steve was a champion in the making and perhaps in this chapter I can add up the factors that give the answer to the question.

Looking at Steve as we see him today, World Champion and television personality, it is very obvious that he comes across as a pleasant lad. He has a good personality and a winning smile. He's got youth on his side and he appeals just as much to the mums and dads as he does to the kids. The newspapers and sponsors took to him immediately, not just because 'everyone loves a winner' but because he has clean-cut good looks, that square jaw . . . there's little to fault in anything about him. He's not a boy of many mannerisms and he is nothing like the image of a snooker player that many people, unfortunately, still have in mind – the old idea that a snooker player is a bit of a sharp character or layabout. Of course, we know that that image is wrong and Steve certainly proves this. He projects a plain, honest attitude.

I know that some players and spectators have criticized Steve's habit of throwing his fist in the air when he wins a match. This is something that

Photos: Dave Muscroft.

hasn't been seen in snooker before, but where did it start? Among the kids on the football terraces. It's gone from there to boxing and tennis. Look at some of the things that tennis players do nowadays. Ten years ago a lady player couldn't have a spot of colour on her dress or she'd be sent off. Times change and the influence of the young can be clearly seen in all these sports. Steve is only a young lad and in this habit he's just like all the other kids. This is his way of exclaiming, 'I've done it!' He's only doing what the younger element in all sports do today. I think that if other players take this as a sign of disrespect they are being rather short-sighted. It's the exuberance of youth, that's all. I was amused to see that one of the critics of this habit was Alex Higgins!

When Steve's at the table and playing this great and difficult game it doesn't matter tuppence whether the newspapers like him or whether he gets a thousand fan letters a month. He's got to *play*. He has the technique, this correct reliable technique that has won my heart more than anything. Through the gift of God he has a sweet cue action which is just out of this world. He's blessed with a temperament that allowed him to listen to his elders when he was young, he has been able to enjoy hours of hard practice without becoming bored, he has the character to live up to the role of World Champion.

What do I mean by technique? Let's really take him apart. He's a tall bony lad. Not a lot of flesh on him. When he bends he bends right from the hips – his body doesn't arch, he goes straight down from the hips – and he's able to look right through the length of the cue. The only time that 99 per cent of players, good bad or indifferent, sight correctly in terms of viewing the shot through the length of the cue is when they use the rest. The reason is that in using the rest they have to look through the length of the cue and they extend the line of aim. Extending the line of aim is an invaluable aid to sighting the correct line of aim and keeping to it. Steve is able to do that on all his shots.

The stance of a snooker player is so important. In Steve's case, and I don't mean this with any disrespect, when he gets down on the shot he looks like a stick insect. He plants his feet very wide apart, which gives him a strong base. His bridge hand on the table forms a tripod and he's as solid as a rock. There's no spare flesh on him to wobble about – he's as fit as a fiddle. I've seen him at the World Championship eating six or eight grapefruit for breakfast before a match. He's like a boxer – he keeps himself lean and hungry.

The greatest attribute Steve has is his cue action. When I talk about his 'sweet cue action' I mean the *pace* of the cue as it travels through. Snooker players generally tend to deliver the last action of the cue very quickly – they get the job over fast. But if you watch Steve you will see that he has the slowest delivery of them all. His final delivery is slow and deliberate. There is no sudden thrust of the cue, no jerkiness. It is so smooth it is like a piston going back and forth, and that ensures that there is no unnecessary movement – the one thing that must be avoided in this game is excess movement.

Applying all this technique to his natural gifts makes Steve such a fabulous player. The proof of it is what puts fear into the hearts of other players – if they leave a long ball on (and when I say a long ball I don't mean a blue off its spot, I mean a ball about 2 feet out from the top pocket with Steve's cue ball perhaps 1 foot off the baulk cushion) he knocks them in, when all the balls are open and the position is such that if he misses he's in trouble. Long potting is the severest test of technique because any error in aim or in cueing is magnified by the time the cue ball reaches the object ball. It may have to travel 10 feet or so and a millimetre of error at the cue-ball end will become a wide margin of error on the long pots. Steve is the greatest long-ball potter I have ever seen. Walter Donaldson, of the forties and fifties era, was reckoned to be a superb long potter but from my own personal observations I can say that he wasn't as good as Steve.

Some people say that Steve is a 'manufactured' player, but when they're on their own practising, all professional players from Alex Higgins down – and no one has greater natural talent than Alex – are doing much more than just knocking balls in. They're worrying, 'Am I doing this right?', or 'Should I be doing that?' They're working on their own technique and trying to make themselves better players. Does the dictionary distinguish between 'make' and 'manufacture'?

Occasionally I overhear a conversation in which someone asserts that Steve must have miraculous eyesight to be able to pot the way he does. I wouldn't be surprised to learn that Steve has only average eyesight. I don't believe that any test would show his eyesight to be much better than that of other players. It's important to have good eyesight: the fairest way to describe it is *healthy* eyesight. The eyes must be flexible enough to cope with different shots. For instance, on a long shot the eyes go from the cue ball to the object ball and back again, maybe four times, maybe as many as eight times. If the eyes can do that and take in the picture *instantly*, adjusting for long focus and short focus, that's all that is required. Healthy eyes will accommodate to focus correctly on every sort of shot. It's more important to consider that the eyes only transmit messages to the brain. I believe that in many ordinary players there is a big gap between what their eyes see and what the brain actually makes of the signal. It's rather like the difference between what you think your eyes have seen and what a camera (which has no brain) actually records. We've all seen trick photographs or tests which demonstrate this.

During my coaching sessions I notice that people will go on doing the same wrong thing in the same wrong way. It's because they 'see' it as right. It may be in their judgment of angles or when they're attempting to strike the centre of the cue ball. If I say to them, 'Well, look, that isn't the centre of the ball, it's *there*,' and move them a fraction to the left or right, their brain may still see that as 'wrong', but if they can educate their eyes and brain to appreciate the reality I am showing them they will

Photo: Dave Muscroft.

be doing the right thing each time. In the beginning it will look wrong to them, but the fortunate ones will develop a better co-ordination between eye and brain and start to 'see' the right things. This sort of 'vision gap' is very common among average players. Top players cannot have it to any great extent and I would say that Steve Davis has it least of all. To him the picture and the message must be instantly 'married' as they reach his brain.

The brain, of course, is tremendously important. There is no doubt that Steve is an intelligent young man and his intellect is another component in the making of a champion. He's a good chess player, he had a good record at school and he's sensible and thoughtful about all aspects of his life and the game of snooker. For example, in the Coral UK Championship in 1980 when referee John Williams absentmindedly lifted the cue ball from the table instead of taking the pink from the pocket, Steve's opponent Alex Higgins had quite a heated debate with the referee as to the consequences of this remarkable lapse. Steve did not simply keep out of the dispute – he upped and left the arena entirely, making sure that the row would not affect his concentration. How many players would have thought of taking this course?

In his play Steve exhibits a logical incisive mind. Most ordinary club players are quite content to pot the ball. Good players want to pot the ball and obtain position for a colour and perhaps the next red. The professional doesn't just want position, he wants an exact position for his next shot and he's probably thinking two or three moves ahead of that. I don't suppose that Steve can plan any further ahead than any other professionals, but he has a great knowledge of the angles and a memory which gives him a great storehouse of set-piece positions. Although I would say that, of all players, Alex Higgins has the greatest knowledge and understanding of angles, I think Steve runs him close. Once he has learned something he doesn't forget it. Steve played a lot of billiards when he was younger and in billiards one must learn all about the angles and the way the cue ball will behave.

Steve's tactical thinking is very strong for such a young man. In this department, what I call 'generalship', I would bracket him with Tony Meo rather than other younger players like Kirk Stevens or Jimmy White who play a more adventurous game, relying less on a well-thought-out 'game plan'. It requires real brain power to out-manoeuvre the toughest and most experienced players in the world, men who have seen and played all the shots that exist.

Steve, I think, has a very disciplined mind. I don't think he ever fools himself. There comes a time in tactical play when the man has to be very severe with himself. Having considered all the possibilities, having taken over a minute to decide upon his shot, the question in his mind must be, 'But will it work out as I plan?' In my experience I would say that there is a small but crucial area where the player decides, 'Yes, I think it will,' but in fact if he were truly honest with himself he would recognize that in playing the shot he was really thinking, 'Yes, I hope it will.' In other words, he has allowed an element of unfounded optimism to lead him into a silly shot. In my view Steve is hardly capable of this sort of wishful thinking. If the shot doesn't 'add up' he doesn't play it. That is intelligence at work.

Confidence is a mental thing. All the ability in the world will not take a player to the greatest heights unless he has a belief in his skills that enables him to use them ruthlessly to the best advantage. Steve shows this very well in his break-building. When he has reached 30 or 40 in the break and there seem to be no obvious balls on to allow him to continue, you will see him – at a time when he can still lose the frame – potting a colour and deliberately playing for a position which presents a terribly difficult next red. He has the confidence to play this sort of 'life-saving' shot because he believes in his ability to pot that ball once he has taken the colour. This absolute confidence can be devastating to the opponent because Steve is calculating that if he misses the shot, his opponent, coming 'cold' to the table, will not pot the difficult red that Steve had deliberately left himself. This sort of position, when it occurs, is one of intensely high pressure and it is demoralizing for the opponent to watch and recognize what Steve is doing. It has a psychological value beyond that shot and that frame.

Steve seems to have enough mental control to remove himself from all the pressures around him, to 'switch off' and relax. I have seen him go back to his seat while his opponent is in play, close his eyes, drop his head on his chest and I watch him and think, 'He's not *here*.' His mind is miles away from the game, and instead of watching and fretting over his opponent's progress he is enjoying a good rest.

He works hard at controlling his mind and his feelings. In this game we spend our lives teaching players not to rush, to take things slowly. That is the only way to success. Steve is very deliberate in this, as could be seen at the Embassy World Championship when he continually left the table during his shot and walked back to his seat to take a tiny sip of water. One exasperated spectator was heard to observe that the World Championship should have been sponsored by the South Yorkshire Water Board rather than Embassy! But look at all the other players: they get up, walk around the table, chalk their cues, puff on the tip, go and look at the shot from the other end. It's all just as time-consuming and it's all done for one reason – to gain thinking time. Steve's method is perhaps more noticeable but I don't suppose it uses up any more time than the others. It works for him, it's within the rules, and he must do what he can to make sure that there is nothing rushed about his game.

Steve has a formidable array of talents at his command, talents which I have seen developing steadily over the last five or six years which made him the most predictable World Champion of recent times. He got the basics right and continued from there. If a player can do that, he can command the heights of this great game. The basics of correct play are all-important and no one will ever succeed without them. Steve makes it all look so easy and, as we know, it just isn't an easy game.

Today he's the World Champion, *the* Steve Davis. But as I watch him I think, 'He'll always be the one and only Steve Davis, but in a sense he's the first Steve Davis. There will be others like him coming along to challenge and overturn the established players.' That is a prospect to which we can all look forward – and the most predictable thing about it is that 'this' Steve Davis will still be at the top, ready and willing to meet all the new challenges of the future.

20
On the road

The busiest professional players spend as much time on the motorways as they do on the table. Away from the glamour of the top championships they make their living by travelling the length and breadth of Britain, appearing in exhibition games in local clubs and halls. Many of the clubs seek no publicity for such engagements as their own limited membership will fill the room, and in many cases it will only be as a result of a local newspaper report the following week that the locals will learn that their favourite snooker star was in their town, perhaps less than 500 yards away.

The 1981–2 season has been proclaimed as the first year in which tournament prize money from sponsors has exceeded £500,000. That money is earned in substantial chunks – for example, the winner of the Jameson Open in September received £20,000 and the runner-up £10,000. A fair share of such prize money is essential to lift a player into the top earnings bracket. But in addition to the fabulous prize money now on offer there is at least another £500,000 earned by a small number of leading players on the exhibition circuit. A rough calculation based on twenty-six working weeks (the rest of the time being taken up by tournaments), with an average of four bookings a week at a fee of £350 each, gives a total of £546,000 shared by the top fifteen players in the highest-earning class.

Many of the players accept more than four bookings per week. Most of them could work six nights a week, but the effort involved and the strain that such a schedule imposes on their family life means that few professionals set out to take so many bookings and those who attempt it usually live to regret it. The pattern was set by Alex Higgins when he won the world title in 1972. He burst into the public consciousness with more impact than any snooker player before him. Everyone wanted to see Alex in action. So the bookings rolled in, at fees which would seem derisory today, and Alex, with no family ties and an insatiable appetite for snooker, went 'on the road' and pulled in the crowds and the money wherever he went. He won every other title in the game but up to the present day he has not recaptured the world crown. This has had no discernible effect on his bookings. He is still the biggest box-office draw in snooker and is only now being challenged by Steve Davis, Cliff Thorburn, Jimmy White and Terry Griffiths as a sure-fire sell-out for any promotion.

It is only in the last two or three years that the professionals and their advisers have realized that it is not necessary to work every hour on the clock to make a living. The evidence had been there in the career of Alex Higgins, but they all ignored it and the accepted wisdom was that a player who won the World Championship had to work every hour God sent in his championship year in order to cash in on his success. So the players accepted every booking offered to them and spent their time dashing around the country living out of suitcases and saying goodnight to their children by telephone. The organization of their diaries was not all that it might have been and most professionals can tell horror stories of doing an exhibition in Bournemouth on Monday, Glasgow on Tuesday and Eastbourne on Wednesday.

The work was there, the money was there, but there had to be a more sensible way of earning it. Some of the players had managers. But almost

Alex Higgins. Photo: Dave Muscroft.

Jackie Rea. Photo: John Carty.

Terry Griffiths watched by Steve Davis. Photo: Dave Muscroft.

anyone who had access to a telephone and claimed he could read and write was qualified to be a manager. The most sensible players looked after their own affairs and built up a steady reliable circuit of bookings, grouped together in areas of the country which they could return to at much the same time every year. Ray Reardon and the former Irish champion Jackie Rea were the most organized and efficient players before snooker entered the millionaire era.

Jackie, who has not had any great tournament successes since the sixties, has always had a highly polished 'cabaret' act and his snooker exhibitions are the most entertaining of all. He is a skilful player, as his vast repertoire of trick shots proves, but he is as much a comedian as a snooker player. His shows never flag for a moment. Whether he is playing club members or doing his hair-raising trick shots he maintains a continuous flow of repartee and Irish wit – half of it in his familiar Irish brogue and half (for reasons best known to himself) in hysterically funny pidgin Chinese. While the fees of the other players have rocketed, Jackie has kept his at a very modest level and has been in constant demand for thirty years and more. Although he can work every night of the week, he makes his travels in a leisurely way and does not have the rat-race pressures of the big tournaments to worry him. Of course his act is more or less the same wherever he goes, but tonight's audience in Cambridge will not be concerned that he told all the same stories last night in Watford. Like the music-hall troupers of old, he relies on live audiences, and like the old comedians his material is not 'killed' overnight by exposure on television. It goes on fresh every night to a new audience who hear his tales and see the tricks for the first time. In truth, some clubs book Jackie three times in a year and such is the strength of his humour that the audiences laugh just as much on the third visit as they did on the first. Many of his shows are presented in the smaller clubs, and with an intimate audience of sixty or seventy people Jackie lets slip a few tales about the professionals of the past and present which would never be heard on television!

Although Dennis Taylor and John Virgo have mastered the art of combining snooker and humour in their exhibitions and are considered to be the top men in that area today, they both owe an enormous debt to Jackie Rea for showing them how it is done. It is no overstatement to say that all professionals who rely on a bit of humorous chat with an audience learned something of that difficult craft from the Irish maestro.

Ray Reardon took a rather different path. As his fame increased and offers of every sort poured in, he could see that he needed professional management to relieve himself and his wife Sue of the burdens of negotiating contracts, especially as, for the first time, these negotiations were with people from outside the fairly limited world of club snooker and involved concepts and plans outside the experience of even the shrewdest player – which Reardon undoubtedly is. It was no longer enough to be able to say, 'Yes, I can be in Scunthorpe on 4 March.' Ray therefore joined forces with John Spencer and they formed a company with Del Simmons, who was no one's idea of a snooker player, but everyone's idea of a manager. That company was the International Snooker Agency and it quickly signed up the world's leading players. The premise was simple: the players would concentrate on playing the game

John Virgo. Photo: John Carty.

Dennis Taylor and fans. Photo: Dave Muscroft.

and Del would concentrate on getting them the money.

There was an immediate bonus in leaving the negotiations to Del. It is either the greatest blessing or the greatest curse of snooker, depending on the player's temperament, that everyone wants to be his friend. One booking in a club and the person who hands over the fee and has a drink with the player is his friend for life. That person will phone the player a year later to book him again saying, 'Hello, John, it's Jim here' – and woe betide John if he does not instantly remember who 'Jim' is. Many a booking has been lost on that brief conversation. When a player acted for himself there could be some embarrassment in discussing the fee. The 'old pals act' generally kept fees down. Del Simmons is nobody's old pal. His duty is to do the best he can for his players and there is no embarrassment for him in hiking up the fees to what he thinks the market can stand.

Before Del came on the scene the market had never been seriously tested. Everyone knew what Spencer, Reardon and Higgins could charge and they made a calculation based on their supposed status in relation to the 'big three'. Ray Reardon was virtually the first player to find himself in constant demand at a time when he had decided to devote more time to his family and accept fewer bookings. He had been everywhere, done everything, and had achieved enough financial security to value an evening at home more than a £200 fee. The tactic was simple: increase his fee by so much that only those clubs which were desperate to have him could afford him. Those who could not afford him could book another ISA client at a lower price. So his fees went up from about £175 a night to over £300. Initially there was a drop in the number of bookings – which was, of course, the desired objective – but very quickly the market rose to meet the new prices and once again an increase was needed to give Ray the odd night off. As this was going on, the fees of other players were rising in line with the leaders' fees. Higgins was still a workaholic and taking every booking that came his way, but with Del representing him his earnings doubled in a year or so.

From about 1977 onwards the bookings from places other than the traditional social clubs increased. Many local authorities had new leisure centres and needed a varied programme to fill them. They turned to snooker. Independent promotors were hiring theatres seating a thousand people and charging up to £5 for admission to snooker tournaments. In these new circumstances the old method of calculating fees went by the board and the match venue became the important factor. The age of the £1,000 fee had arrived.

It is a lot of money in anyone's language, but the reasoning was simple: the players had become entertainers comparable to singers or other showbusiness types – and showbusiness fees had long been above this level. Then too, the managers could easily count the gate. If one thousand people were to pay £4 each and the players were paid at the old club level, who was to benefit? Promoters who may have had no previous connections with

Steve Davis. Photo: Dave Muscroft.

snooker? No chance, said Del Simmons and the other managers. Pay the players £1,000 each and you still have a reasonable profit.

In fact the typical large-audience promotion is an afternoon and evening job, but since most of the players have little use for their afternoons other than to play golf they don't consider this to be extra work. As late as 1980, one manager was caught out by failing to ask for details of the venue. A promotor wished to stage a three-man all-day tournament. Each of the three (quite junior) players had different managers. Two of the players had been signed at £550 each for the day. The other had been booked at his routine fee of £90. The promotor queried this fee twice and was assured that it was correct. Came the day and nine hundred people in the north of England paid a total of over £2,500 to see the matches. The result? The £90 player beat the other two to win the cup! No amount of heated debate and explanation could satisfy the 'successful' player. He has a new manager now.

The club and exhibition circuit that was once described as the 'bread and butter' of the professional player now provides jam and cream as well – but at a cost. The players have to travel most of the day and spend their nights and some of their daylight hours in anonymous hotel rooms. The trick is to establish a network of friends around the country. Every player would rather stay in a congenial private home than in an hotel. Just as Her Majesty's judges have residences to accommodate them while on the Crown Court circuit, so too the top players have welcoming homes (one might almost, in the language of spies, call them 'safe houses') where they may rest in comfort. As these houses generally belong to the well-heeled, there is usually a table in the house and the professional will practise or play a few relaxed frames with his host and his friends into the early hours. In a sense he 'sings for his supper', but it is infinitely preferable to the plastic hotels and gut-rotting motorway food.

As the big tournaments now account for so much of the professional's time, he has fewer opportunities to take exhibition bookings. There are periods in the year when all the top players are in Canada or Australia for two weeks at a time. In the past these overseas trips could be confined to the summer months when there was little activity in Britain, but such are the demands of the game today that overseas countries can now offer highly attractive tournaments in the middle of the British season. If the clubs cannot book anyone in the top twenty during that time, they must book someone lower down in the rankings. Thus the benefits of all the increased activity filter down through the system and bring prosperity to the unfashionable or less successful players. The great strength of the system is that even these players will put on a show to leave the audience spellbound. They have been raised in a hard school, their skills far surpass the ordinary club members they are called upon to play, and even a limited repertoire of trick shots will have an appreciative audience begging for more.

For a gregarious, outgoing character who has no family to think about it is a pleasant way to earn £50,000 a year. But not all snooker players are born gregarious characters. Some of them suffer agonies in learning to face a live audience. They all have to school themselves to speak naturally and clearly in the smoke-filled rooms. They learn to chat with the committee members in the bar; to turn the other cheek as the 'experts' in the audience make offensive comments on their standard of play; to explain for the thousandth time what sort of cue they use. Because they are professionals and this is their work. Because in their hearts this is where they come from and this is where they live. Because the show must go on. And at the end of the night, having made a record break or having lost to an unknown amateur, having made new friends or lost some old ones, they return to the Jaguar, Daimler or Volvo and while their audience sleeps they face 300 miles of hard road.

Tomorrow it's Hartlepool.

21
The amateur scene

It may be thought that the organized amateur side of snooker is no more than a proving ground for the professional players of tomorrow. From the point of view of an ambitious young player that is partly true, but it is far from being the whole truth. There are thousands of players around the world who can play this game at a very high standard and even today, with the hordes storming the gates of the WPBSA, the serious amateur player who wishes to remain an amateur is still in the majority.

As has been mentioned before, snooker is an 'open' sport and the man commonly called an 'amateur' (but more correctly, if clumsily, called a 'non-professional') can earn a fair amount of money in prizes and exhibition fees in the course of a year. For a leading amateur with an attractive style, prepared to put himself out by travelling to all the various events, £3,000 a year would be a reasonable target these days. A few years ago there was so much activity at the top of the amateur game and so little prospect of reward for a new professional that players stayed 'amateur' longer than they do today.

There are very many tournaments where a player can pick up a first prize of £300 or £500 for a weekend's play, but of course these sums pale into insignificance when compared with the money in the professional game. It is difficult to tell a really good amateur to wait another year to turn pro when he can see his friend Dave Martin on television receiving £5,000 for reaching the semi-final of the Jameson International Open.

It is the most obvious feature of snooker today that the vast amounts of money available in the professional game have created a pressure on more and more players to turn professional. The Welsh and the Irish still have experienced senior players at the top but England and Scotland are left with few indeed. So the big money has had an effect. How far does the amateur game affect the professional scene? Although the amateur game has produced all the professional players of any note, it would be wrong to say that the professional game depends directly upon it. It's rather like having a parachute in an aeroplane – it's insignificant when it's not needed, but if it wasn't there . . . ?

The game as a whole needs a strong amateur side

Photos: John Carty.

Left: Les Dodd (Southport), Merseyside's leading amateur, winner of the area title, the Plessey Invitation and the Greenall Whitley Open in 1981. He made his debut for England in October, but was not at his best. A great joker and smiler, he has ambitions to turn professional which will surely be realized.
Right: Ian Williamson (Leeds) was one of Britain's leading juniors but suffered a two-year loss of form until 1980. He was British Junior Champion from 1975 to 1977 and Junior Billiards Champion in 1976–7. A slow, methodical player, he has returned to form in 1981 and reached the semi-finals of the William Youngers Open at Leeds and the final of the Pontins Open at Prestatyn.

and we may reflect upon the state of the amateur game at this time when the professionals have never had it so good. Money is just as important to the amateurs, but regrettably there is a lot less of it. The main reason is that outside Wales, Scotland and a few regions of England, television coverage of amateur snooker is unknown and without television the really big sponsorship money cannot be obtained. There are, nevertheless, many sponsors in the amateur game and this has helped to maintain much regional activity. At the national level Wales does very well with its arrangement with Woodpecker Cider, and England has had major tournaments courtesy of State Express and Saccone & Speed but has not yet found sponsors for its premier championships, the English and the English Counties. In Canada increasing numbers of sponsors have been found at the local level, and the Dufferin Cue company is still a major sponsor.

The amateur game only exists through the efforts of hundreds of local officials and organizers and the

Left: Wayne Jones, a twenty-three-year-old from Rumney, South Wales, won the very tough Welsh qualifying section of the English Championship to appear in the Southern Area Finals in London. In his first round he beat Dorset-based Dave Chalmers but lost in the next round to Irishman Paul Ennis. Wayne was Welsh Boys Champion in 1975, British Boys Champion in 1976 (in which he beat Jimmy White), and was runner-up in the British Junior in 1977. He was Welsh Youth Champion in 1979 and 1980. He has a highest break of 136 and hopes to turn professional. Played for Wales in 1981.
Right: Norman Dagley of Hinckley is considered to be one of the best billiard players in the world, amateur or professional. Despite the recent modest revival in professional billiards he has remained an amateur, and in Delhi in late 1981 he sought to win the World Amateur Billiards title for the third time. He won the English Championship nearly every year in the seventies, being rivalled only by Bobby Close of Hartlepool. Throughout the world of amateur billiards only Close, Michael Ferreira of India and Paul Mifsud of Malta can threaten his dominance. He is a brilliant player who must soon be tempted into the professional ranks to see if he can repeat his record of success there. Photos: John Carty.

strength of snooker in any given area is related to the numbers of such officials and their level of ability. The world governing body, the B&SCC, has a small paid staff, but it too must rely on unpaid officials and it is becoming clear that they need more staff and more voluntary effort if they are to take full advantage of all the available opportunities. National associations around the world must have the people and the money to maintain national teams and to send representatives to the gold riband events, the World Amateur Snooker and the World Amateur Billiards Championships. Through the sponsorship and assistance of Pontins, the Home International series is no longer a financial headache, but the World Amateur Championships are daunting prospects for all countries.

Despite the difficulties, the condition of the amateur game is quite sound. It could be much better, but the players tend to get the quality of administration they deserve. The average snooker player would rather saw a foot off his cue than sit on a committee, so he leaves it to others. The professionals, it will be noted, do it themselves. If all the best players will not give some of their time and attention to how the game is run, they can hardly complain if it is not run as well as they would like. But the real strength of the game is in the players: not in their organizing ability, but their talents and skills on the table. The amateur game must have its stars. They are still around but we do not have a 'golden age' such as we had in the period 1975–7 when John Virgo, Willie Thorne, Patsy Fagan, Terry Griffiths, Alwyn Lloyd and Ray Edmonds were at the top of the amateur tree, playing each other all over the country in what seemed to be a perpetual round of big matches.

The goal for every player, whether he is on his way to the professional ranks or not, is to be called to play for his country. There are some inconsistencies in the selection of teams and not every man who deserves a place gets one, but generally the national team reflects the very best of the year's amateur talent.

One of the players who did not get the call for England, and who was also refused admission by the professionals, is Mick Fisher of Bedford. Since

Left: George Wood of Felling, County Durham. He has become one of England's most respected amateurs, a regular in the England team and the leading snooker player from the North-East of England. He is an attacking player who also has an intelligent safety game. A family man with no immediate plans to become a professional, he will continue to pick up some of the biggest prizes in snooker. In 1981, with Mike Darrington, he represented England in a playing tour of Zimbabwe.
Right: Dave Gilbert of London, one of England's most promising players, had a devastating setback when, in October 1980, he was seriously injured in a motorway accident in which his younger sister died. He was out of action for six months and although his broken bones mended, the damage to his cueing arm was such that he will never be able to straighten it. Fortunately that is the arm that never needs to be straight and Dave has adapted well. He won an open tournament in London, reached the quarter-finals of the Pontins Open and the final of the Lucania National. He has established himself once more as one of London's best senior players.

Photos: John Carty.

THE AMATEUR SCENE

Left: Mike Darrington of High Wycombe, Bucks, has dominated the Home Counties area for many years, having been champion six times. He was late to find favour with the England selectors, first appearing for England in 1979, but he has had a fine international record since then. In 1981 he reached the final of the Guinness Open, losing to Steve Davis. He had a sound record in tournaments around the country, but has kept apart from the trend in London to have tournaments starting at midnight and ending at ten in the morning. 'I'll leave that to the youngsters,' laughed Mike, 'I'm too old for that!' He has been one of England's most successful and well-rewarded amateurs of recent years and it is unlikely that he will turn professional – although, of course, he could if he chose to.

Right: John Hargreaves of Stoke-on-Trent has been an England international for so long that he pre-dates many of the officials! He is extravagantly thin, extremely polite and in both his looks and manner seems to belong to the thirties rather than the eighties. He is the outstanding 'gentleman' of snooker players, but with a cue in his hand he is about as reticent as a cobra looking for its lunch. Probably the hardest man in England to beat in a match, he has upset the plans of more 'rising stars' than anyone. Those players who do beat him count it as one of their biggest successes. He won the Skol Tournament in 1981 and was an outstanding player for the England team. Photos: John Carty.

he first came to prominence in 1974 when he reached the Southern Area Final (losing to Patsy Fagan), he has had a consistent record of success, reached many finals around the country and won some big tournaments. As owner of the Greyfriars Snooker Centre in Bedford he has been able to attract the best players to his club and he has had wins over Fred Davis, Terry Griffiths and Dennis Taylor. He has been playing near-neighbour Willie Thorne in challenge matches for years and some alarming sums of money have changed hands on these results. They tend to play 'home and away' between Bedford and the Willie Thorne Snooker Centre in Leicester, and the score in this marathon series is about level. Mick is a fine player and a distinguished amateur and in losing out on selection for England and for admission to the professional game he could be rated as the unluckiest player of the year.

The title of 'Player of the Year' – not that there is one outside of the London and Home Counties area – must go to Bob Harris of Wimbledon who won more one-day and two-day tournaments than anyone. From a rather chequered early career as a good player he emerged in 1979–80 as a young man likely to step into the star category. The twenty-six-year-old Bob won the Courage Open, reached the final of the Southern Area (making an English Championship official record break of 123), won the London Open, the first Midnight Masters at Kingston, the Strachan West of England Championship, the Southall Masters and the Lucania National Championship. As well as being a very talented and exciting player to watch, he is a personable young man, very attractive to the opposite sex and he'll make a fortune when he gets that face on television! His image is that of a latter-day John Travolta – with some justification, as he has been a male model and professional disco dancer in his time. On and off the table he is rather strong on style. He is famous for his white suits (before Kirk Stevens!) and Panama hats, and despite his record of success his reputation as 'Flash Bob', a name by which he is known throughout the country without mention of his surname, still sticks. He detests both the nickname and the image, fearing that he will not be seen as a serious player. But he is all of that. His game is reminiscent of John

Left: Bill Oliver of Plymouth is the owner of the Pot Black Snooker Centre in his home town and one of the very few senior players to come to the fore in 1981. With his partner Roger Cole he won the Guinness National Pairs Championship in May and in October he won one of the biggest events in snooker, the Pontins Open. That win gave him the highest prize of his life, nearly £2,000, and established him as one of England's new stars. He has not yet played for England, having been just another county player before his successes of 1981, but if he maintains his winning ways the selectors will have to consider him. He is an attractive player, a great potter and a very cheerful and modest man – the epitome of the ideal amateur snooker player. Bill Oliver will remember 1981!

Right: Bob Harris of Wimbledon (see left and above for details of his career).

Photos: John Carty.

Left: Leon Heywood, a twenty-eight-year-old from Adelaide, Australia, enjoyed a short visit to England in 1981. He was the first Australian amateur to make a 147 break (in 1979) and has represented his country in the World Amateur Championship. While in England he was constantly and surprisingly asked for autographs – until it transpired that the fans thought he was Kirk Stevens! So he cheerfully signed them 'Kirk Stevens'.
Right: New Zealand's Dene O'Kane (see below for details of his career).
Photos: John Carty.

Spencer at his best, with power potting and sheer flair the notable characteristics. Bob is now a match-hardened player both in official tournaments and in hair-raising money matches. He was picked to play for England in 1981 and won all his international matches. Having waited to fulfil his amateur commitments, he 'missed the boat' in applying for professional status and had to wait for the WPBSA meeting of May 1982. But he will get in and he will get on. Natural talent and star quality like his cannot be held back.

One of the most interesting players to make his mark in 1981 was Dene O'Kane of New Zealand. The eighteen-year-old Dene was born in Christchurch but has lived most of his life in Auckland. He came over to England to appear on 'Junior Pot Black' and stayed to improve his snooker. He was based at Kingston Snooker Centre and soon proved that he was the equal of the British when he won the Marina Classic tournament at Plymouth. He followed that with a win in a big event at Kingston and the blasé London fans freely admitted that here was another star. Before his move to England he had won ten or eleven tournaments in New Zealand and in September 1980 he became the youngest-ever winner of the New Zealand Championship. This win guaranteed him one of the two New Zealand places in the World Amateur Snooker Championship in Calgary, Canada, in 1982.

Dene started to play snooker at the age of twelve, using a table-tennis table covered with a rug and golf balls instead of snooker balls. He studied from books and developed the basic skills, and even with the rug and the golf balls he practised seriously for hours on end. In time he bought a proper cue and acquired a set of snooker balls, but he still had no contact with other good players – or indeed any players. He watched the World Amateur Billiards Championship in Auckland in 1975 which Norman Dagley won: 'That really sparked my interest when I saw what could be done in proper conditions,' said Dene.

His local billiard hall was the Takapuna Snooker Room, but players under the age of eighteen were not admitted. Dene used to hang around outside and one day, on his way to buy fireworks for Guy Fawkes night, he was spotted by the club marker, Sam Lemmone, himself a good player, who recognized the look of longing in Dene's eye. Sam invited Dene in to play a few shots. By this time he was quite adept and he impressed Sam, so he was allowed to use their tables regularly, 'but the police kept throwing me out', said Dene.

In his first year on real tables his highest break was 78 and he played some of the leading local players like Grant Hayward, Peter Crookenden and Alan Dreaver, who has now moved to Australia. The Takapuna is still Dene's home club and it is the centre of many big-money matches in Auckland. Dene mentions another of the local stars, Mike Turoa: 'His wife Evelyn is a brilliant player. If she went to the UK she would do really well against the best women players.'

Dene is sure that his stay in the UK has improved his game: 'I'm 10 or 14 points better since I stepped off the plane,' he said. In October 1981 he made his lifetime best break, a 139, at Kingston. Although he is certain to represent New Zealand in Calgary, Dene is obliged to return to New Zealand early in

J. R. Wedge (left) and Ken Shea of Canada.
Photo: Bob Hargrove.

THE AMATEUR SCENE

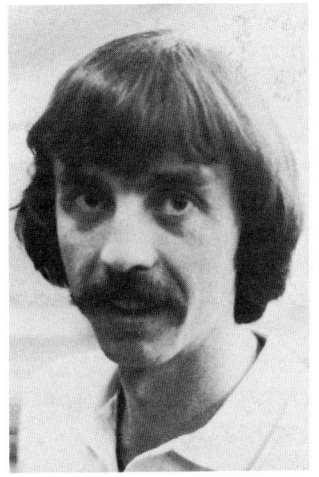

Left: Pat White of Windsor, Ontario.
Right: Frank Cavaliere of Toronto, finalist in the 1981 Ontario Championship.
Photos: Graham Duncan.

1982 to play off against 1981 champion Glen Kwok to decide who will be number one player. It seems a long way to go to settle this issue but, as Dene says, 'I'll be able to go at a time when some of the biggest tournaments are on. One of them has a first prize of $1,500 and I'll have a chance to make some nice money when I do go home.'

Dene is a follower of the Guru Maharaj Ji and he spends at least four hours each day in meditation. He has been interested in these teachings for nearly two years and the movement has millions of members around the world. 'It's not a religion,' he says. 'The word "religion" stems from "realization" and the one true realization is the experience of God. I'm into it to be happy and to fulfil the purpose of life.' He has been known to slip into a trance in the middle of a conversation but fortunately (the rules of snooker being silent on the point) has never done so during a match. There is no doubt that his beliefs are deeply and sincerely held; there is equally no doubt that Dene is the best young prospect to have come out of New Zealand. The only doubt over the career of this polite and intelligent young man lies in the insight and self-knowledge that he credits to the teachings of the guru: 'To tell the truth, I'm more into this than I am into snooker.'

In Canada the advances made in the last few years continue. The start of the 1981 season was a big disappointment to the Canadian public in that the international tournament normally held at the Canadian National Exhibition in Toronto could not be staged. Although the exhibition has been valuable as a site for this important tournament in the past, it was far from ideal and the promoter, Terry Haddock, needed a new venue to improve and develop this major event. Although he found sponsors and television coverage it ultimately proved impossible to set any date that would suit the top UK professionals – because the tournament scene in Britain is so busy – and the Canadian Open had to be postponed.

The main focus of interest in Canada is the World Amateur Snooker Championship, which the Canadian Association will host in Calgary in October 1982. Two of the Canadian players in this are already known: Jim Bear, the 1980 champion and Robert Chaperon, the 1981 champion. As host country Canada is likely to have more than the usual two representatives, and in order to ensure that the country's other players are known, the Canadian Amateur Championship for 1981 has had to be telescoped and each of the most successful players in this will have a chance of becoming one of the additional players in the World Amateur.

The organization of Canadian snooker is becoming more efficient, with the hall owners and the billiard trade playing an increasing part in supporting tournaments. In Ontario, for example, amateur events of one kind or another are scheduled for most weekends throughout the season. Ontario organizer Graham Duncan calculates that the level of activity is double what it was in 1980–1. Canadian snooker is still not very successful in attracting sponsors from outside the business, however, mainly because the press and television give no coverage to the amateur game.

With the best of the Canadian professionals based in England, there was little action on the professional scene in their home country. The Canadian Professional Championship, sponsored by Dufferin Cue, was scheduled for the end of December 1981, but fell through for various reasons. One of the home-based professionals, Bernie Mikkelsen, kept his hand in by making his

Left: Steve Wilson of Ottawa.
Right: Scarboro's Gino Rigitano, who made breaks of 128 and 102 in the Toronto qualifying area of the Ontario Championship.
Photos: Graham Duncan.

Left: Robert Chaperon (Sudbury), Ontario Amateur and Canadian Amateur Champion.
Right: Joe Silva (Hamilton) who scored the only century, a 102, in the competition proper of the Ontario Championship.
Photos: Graham Duncan.

eleventh maximum break at Le Spot, Scarboro, in September, while Sue LeMaich became the second woman to make a century break when she made a 102 at the Golden Cue in Hamilton, Ontario. The 1981 Amateur Champion, Robert Chaperon, won the title by beating Carey Lorraine of Winnipeg, and earlier in the year he had also won the Canadian Billiards title. Unfortunately for him, national funds were not sufficient to send him to India in November 1981 to compete in the World Amateur Billiards Championship in Delhi.

A number of other top players emerged from the increased number of competitions held. Gino Rigitano of Scarboro won some good-quality tournaments and showed consistent form throughout the year.

In Eastern Canada J. R. Wedge of St John, New Brunswick, retained his Canadian Maritimes title, beating another top Canadian and 1979 champion Ken Shea of Dartmouth in the final. A new face in this tournament was Marcel Guilbault of St John, who took third place, beating John McCoombs (Dartmouth) to earn a place in the Canadian Championship. But defeated finalist Ken Shea had another big success during the year – his Ottawa team consisting of himself, Erwin Budge and Bill Olson won the International Snooker League in Miami, Florida, beating Scotland into second place and leaving England third. This tournament, now in its seventh year, was organized by Bobby Miller of the Bermudan Snooker Association and the individual champion of the series was the man who helped to start it all, Noel Miller-Cheevers of England.

There will always be problems of geography in organizing Canadian snooker, but despite the difficulties the amateur game is clearly thriving. One other development in 1981 may have an indirect effect on it: in November 1981 it was announced that E. J. Riley Ltd., the biggest company in the billiard trade, had bought a half-share in the Ontario Billiard Supply Co., which trades under the name of 'World of Billiards' from Toronto. Riley became the first company to extend its activities overseas. With centres in Toronto, Calgary, Edmonton and Vancouver, it has a national network to supply its sixteen different table models and all its other stock. Riley chairman Alan Deal became a director of the company and former sole owner Mike Holubik, a well-known figure in Canadian snooker, remains as chief executive. A strong trade usually means a strong game and in the UK the Riley company has been a valuable sponsor and supporter of amateur snooker. If it maintains that policy in Canada, the amateurs could do well out of the new deal.